THE
COMPLETE BOOK
—— OF ——
WATER
GARDENING

THE COMPLETE BOOK
OF
WATER GARDENING

An Inspirational Guide
William Rae-Smith

BRACKEN BOOKS

THE COMPLETE BOOK OF WATER GARDENING
is published 1989 by Bracken Books
an imprint of Bestseller Publications Ltd.,
Princess House, 50 Eastcastle Street,
London W1N 7AP, England.

ISBN 1 85170 289 X

The Complete Book of Water Gardening
was conceived, edited, designed and
produced for Bracken Books Ltd. by
Morgan Samuel Editions
4 Somerset Road, London W13 9PB.

Editorial: Emma Worth, Paul Graham
Design: Tony Paine, Sarah Macdonald
Illustrations: Jim Robins
Picture research: Jane Lewis
Publisher: Nigel Perryman

Typeset in 10/13pt and 9/12pt Quorum by Highbridge Printing, London
Separations by Scantrans, Singapore
Printed and bound by Slovart, Czechoslovakia

CONTENTS

FOREWORD

Gardening is one of the most popular pastimes in the world. Partly, no doubt, this is because we all have a deep-rooted instinct to nurture plants, dating back to the days — not so long ago — when people had no alternative but to grow crops in order to eat, and to nurture herbs in order to cure their ailments.

The popularity of gardening is also, undoubtedly, due to the unique opportunity it gives for the gardener to create a restful and pleasing environment: one that provides a peaceful area for relaxation and quiet contemplation. But this is not the full story, for gardening is also an art, which gives people a chance to design and shape areas of landscape and make personal statements about relationships with nature.

The use of water in the garden is at the least helpful, and probably essential, if one is to realize any of these opportunities. Water has so many different and contrasting qualities, all of which can be put to use to achieve the effect you desire. In one garden, it can be a calm reflective surface, tranquil and peaceful; in another, it can crash resoundingly through an arrangement of rocks, or shoot towards the sky in a foaming, bubbling jet. In a more sophisticated garden, water can play its part in the overall effect of a modern sculpture, or, through symbolism, recall a philosophy of life.

For an art that opens up so many possibilities, the techniques of water gardening are not at all hard to master. Modern materials, such as butyl pool liners, pre-formed pools, aerated fountain nozzles and pumps that can work underwater, have brought a wide range of possibilities within the scope of the amateur. So much of the hard work and ingenuity on which the water gardeners of history relied is made redundant, and a water garden is within the scope of most gardeners; nor is space an essential prerequisite: a restrained Japanese-style water garden can add meaning to even the smallest town garden.

What is important to the would-be water gardener, though, is a sense of design and of the importance of water as a design element. Since the first water gardens were built, around 3,000BC, water has had a spiritual and philosophical importance, as well as a practical purpose, in the garden as in life and religion. Over the years, a set of basic principles have evolved, which try to define the various ways of using water and what these imply. The first section of this book — THE PRINCIPLES OF WATER GARDENING — attempts to set down these principles, and suggest ways in which they can be applied to your garden.

The principles of water gardening are by no means rigid and inflexible, however. The second section — THE WATER GARDEN TRADITION — shows how they have been changed, refined and manipulated by different cultures, each of which has created its own tradition of water gardening — one that reflects its philosophy, spirituality, its practical needs, and, sometimes, its sense of humour.

I hope that these two sections will open up a world of possibilities for the use of water in your garden, and allow you to come up with a design that reflects your personality and priorities. Once you have decided on this, the last section — WATER GARDEN TECHNIQUES — will show you how to put your ideas into practice.

Whatever style of water garden you decide is right for you, I hope that the end result gives you as much pleasure as the art of water gardening gives me.

William Rae-Smith
London and Vaucluse, April 1989

THE PRINCIPLES OF WATER GARDENING

INTRODUCTION
An Inspiration and Life Force; Roots in Water; Religion
and Symbolism; Water in the Garden.

STILL WATER
Animation — Europe, Languid Stourhead, Animating
Your Pool; Containment — Islamic Restraint, Space and
Serenity, Precise Lines, Raised Pools and Borders;
Reflections — Reflections on Your Pool.

MOVING WATER
Cascades and Waterfalls — The Natural Waterfall;
Fountains — Fountains as Symbols and in Religion;
The Fountain as Art.

The canal at Westbury Court, near Gloucester, still
reflects light at dusk, forming a mysterious visual
link with the horizon.

INTRODUCTION

AN INSPIRATION AND LIFE-FORCE

M any years ago, the arid heat of the desert breathed life into the sophisticated water gardens of Islam. Water became the inspiration of Islamic art, which reflected a deep appreciation for its purity and its life-giving properties. This appreciation is rarely evident today, when daily contact with water usually involves a mundane household chore. In modern industrial society the great rivers and oceans of our world are often taken for granted, abused and polluted. But the art of water gardening is inseparable from the historical uses and applications of water, and from the philosophical and spiritual systems that have grown up around water since the dawning of civilization: each element has made its contribution to the changing synthesis that lies behind the use of water for our relaxation and pleasure.

ROOTS IN WATER

The boundless desert sands appear to be beyond life, growth, time or sound. The searing wind sculpts a sinister parody of pastoral tranquillity among the dunes, with mock carvings of lakes and streams, hills and valleys, and even leisurely paths and graceful bridges. But without water, this enormous sculpture can never be more than a huge restless body of dust, encompassing over a fifth of the world's desert.

With water, however, everything has meaning. The dust of decay can be moulded to form the bricks of civilization; likewise, living cells can grow and reproduce. So water is the source of life, altering landscapes and shaping peoples. Without food, life can be sustained for months, but without water, for only days. In fact, each of us starts our life surrounded by water; for months, babies in the womb are aware of the gentle, soothing ebb and flow of the fluid in which they swim.

Our roots in water are not just physiological, though, for water is essential for every aspect of human evolution. Each great culture started its development next to a great river: Chinese civilization evolved along the

A poignant sculpture, by David Wynne, lends a
graceful poetry to this still pond at Easton Grey
House.

banks of the *Yellow River;* the Ancient Egyptians spread outward from the *Nile*; the Indians from the *Indus* and the Persians from the *Tigris* and *Euphrates*. The flow of a river, suggesting a spring and a bourn, a beginning and an end, must have acted as a chronometer and an inspiration, a testimony to the passing of time.

Ancient man soon learnt that his development was determined by his capacity to organize and manipulate water. His first step was to develop a means of irrigating the rich alluvial plains beside rivers, thereby guaranteeing and increasing the harvest; he also quickly learnt how to use water for transport and defence.

One of the most interesting methods of primitive irrigation was the Qanat. By excavating a tunnel from a village to the subterranean water level at the base of the mountain, the ingenious ancient Persians tapped fresh water and brought it to the arid plateau where it was needed. From the air, one can see today the crater-like holes that ventilated the tunnels dug from the foot of a mountain to a distant village.

RELIGION AND SYMBOLISM

As a natural consequence to its importance to early societies, water came to play an integral part in religion and its rituals. It features frequently in the familiar Bible stories: The Great Flood that washed away evil, for example; Moses parting the Red Sea; the rite of Baptism; Jesus walking on water; the transformation of water into wine. This ritual use of water is not confined to Judaism and Christianity, but is a feature of many other religions — Hindus, for instance, practise ritual bathing before religious ceremonies.

In some theologies, though, purification through water was also associated with death. To the Romans, the River *Styx* symbolized the barrier between life and death. A coin was placed in the mouth of the dead as payment for the boatman Charon, who shipped them across the river to the underworld — a journey into the unknown. Viking dead were laid out on lavishly decorated ships to sail on a mystical voyage across the oceans to seek out a holy destination; after his death, King Arthur was placed on a barge by Sir Bedivere and escorted across the water by mysterious fair ladies to the magical Island of Avalon.

Water is often considered a feminine quality, associated with fertility. This is especially true in the Oriental concept of Yin and Yang. The former represents the soft, yielding nature of water — the common portrayal of femininity; and the latter signifies the hard and uncompromising, associated with mountains and masculinity. These categories are also apparent in

A light mist seeps over the tranquil waters of
Faringdon House, in Berkshire.

Greek mythology, in beautiful water nymphs who dote on their handsome heroes and in the masculine portrayal of Neptune, who rules over them, armed with a trident.

The Greeks believed that each stream was the home of a water spirit, so crossing water was a serious business. A bridge was considered a violation of the spirit's domain, and archaeology has revealed how women and children were buried in their foundations in order to appease the spirits. Adapted to a different civilization, the same belief has persisted to modern times: in folklore, witches are unable to cross running water and cannot pursue a victim beyond the water's edge.

Over the ages, each of the many spiritual associations has taken its place as a stone in the ever-changing mosaic of the symbolism of water. It is almost a cliche of poetry that water is the "mirror to the soul". But like all cliches, it contains an element of the truth. Perhaps this is why different people — and different peoples - see so many confused and contradictory images in water: birth or death; joy or sorrow; loss and fulfilment — which one depends on time, place, mood and tradition. To generalize, though, there are five elements in the symbolism of water: baptism and the giving of life, purification and death, the idea of a voyage and the unknown, femininity and fertility and, finally, truth.

WATER IN THE GARDEN

Because the symbolism, the properties and the associations of water are so deeply rooted in the sub-conscious, there is a mysterious comfort to be obtained from the presence of water in daily life — and, practically, that means in the garden. Its presence, brings out a primitive creativity in us, an endless curiosity. Part of the fascination may lie in water's unlimited potential to surprise and delight, because depending on its volume, its temperature and its form, water offers a myriad of different possibilities that stimulate both mind and senses. Even in the simplest of forms, such as a tub-pond or a Japanese *tsukubai*, water will bring a feeling of life and significance into even the most barren of spots. And, of course, it will attract animal life: dragonflies, birds, fish and frogs.

From the aesthetic viewpoint, water is a diverse and fascinating medium for artistic expression, and one that has been manipulated in a variety of ways throughout the history of garden design. The designer can exploit its properties of reflection and sound, its calming influence and its purity. Alternatively, the water garden can be the home of exotic plants, or a liquid extension of the architecture of the house.

Seemingly forgotten, mosses, ferns and moisture-
loving plants flourish among the ancient stone
buttresses of the Pompeian Wall of the Italianate
Gardens of Hever Castle, in Kent.

On a more intimate level, a simple pond can be a self-contained microcosm of existence, where the horticulturalist can cultivate an enormous range of plants to perfect his garden; the dreamer can become absorbed in thought, lulled by the silken rustle of running water that blocks out the intrusive sound of the outside world and heightens the sense of peace and privacy within. But once more, we must return, of necessity, to the indefinable qualities of water. For it is these that make a water garden so strangely attractive, offering, even within the restricted area of a small town garden, the possibility of escape from the hubbub of modern life, and a sequestered spot in which to relax.

To be truly inspiring, though, a water garden must be designed with respect and understanding. Each garden tradition has a concept of the particular form water should take, depending to a great extent on the environment. However, cultural and horticultural traditions have often borrowed from each other, and today we have many types of water garden from which to choose. All these different traditions have had to address the same principles that govern the use of water in a garden: animation, containment, reflection and movement.

The aquaduct at the Old Mill House, in
Nottinghamshire, spans the hushed calm of the
sunlit River Poulter.

STILL WATER

ANIMATION

The Islamic tradition of garden design give us a fine example of how the many properties of water can be used to enhance contemplative and sensual pleasure. The water performs all kinds of technical feats, appearing in copious jets and hesitant drips, in running channels and sparkling crystalline waterfalls. But in spite of the movement in water, one always senses its languidness and peacefulness. The secret of Islamic water design lies in the simultaneous representation of stillness and movement. Water design depends on a careful juxtaposition of both these aspects, so that they complement, rather than detract from each other. Without this enhancement, neither the spirit of water, nor indeed the spirit of the viewer, can be successfully animated. This sense of animation is fundamental to every design feature.

The Islamic climate is not always the best setting for still water, as the heat can make it seem stagnant and lifeless. The pool in the Court of Myrtles in the Alhambra, in Spain, escapes this fate, however. The large expanse of water is set off by two small fountains, and a delicate stream of water, emanating from a long tongue, serves to juxtapose the contrasting qualities of water, creating ripples on the surface of an otherwise motionless pool. This subtle technique, preserving an overall effect of stillness, while at the same time animating the water, exemplifies a combination of confidence and sensitive understanding that is essential for good water design.

The great basins of water, used in the ritual performance of religious ablutions, also demonstrate an interesting visual phenomenon. The surface of the water is quite still, but because the basin is brim-full it seems constantly on the brink of overflowing.

EUROPE

In 17th-century Europe, Andre le Nôtre designed the immense and awe-inspiring water gardens at Versailles and Vaux le Vicomte. A pageant of

The circular pool at Hidcote, in Gloucestershire,
set serenely in a framework of hedges and trees.

fountains jubilantly interspersing large still sheets of water is as impressive as the grand buildings themselves. At Versailles, the *parterres d'eau* were heralded as a new innovative phase in the use of water - a strong contrast with frothing fountains, they highlighted instead the possibilities of passive water in garden design. In time they came to be seen as an inspirational adaptation of water to the northern climate.

The most significant thing about these rectangular pools was their formal containment in an open setting. Unlike previous examples, such as the Court of Myrtles where the pool is enclosed by architecture, the *parterres d'eau* were completely open to natural light, reflecting the changing sky instead of buildings. Within the formal frame of the pool, the surface became a theatre of dramatic forces, of billowing clouds and piercing streaks of sunlight. The reflective properties of water here take on a cosmic scale, bringing the sky to earth and the earth to sky. This was surely the conscious desire of Louis XIV, the Sun King, whose pride and aspiration to become one with the heavens brings to mind Icarus, flying heavenwards on wings of wax.

In 18th-century England, passive water was used in a very different way in the naturalistic garden. The French garden style found little support in this moody land of fluid contour and low cloud, and instead of adopting this new taste in formal gardens the English evolved their own informal style. Rather than containing water in a formal frame, the English modelled the water feature on natural shape. The water was placed at the lowest point of the landform cradled by gentle slopes, whereas at Versailles it was raised up in basins. Used in this way it reflected not only the moods of the sky but the silhouettes of hills and the rich colours of seasonal change.

LANGUID STOURHEAD

Nowhere can the English style be seen better than at Stourhead, where the blazing reflections of autumnal leaves and of flowering rhododendrons attract admiring crowds. In the English landscape style, water gave form a context. The irregular shape and contour, the ungeometric pattern of trees, shrubs and hills in the landscape garden were given a sense of scale and unity. This idea is not unique to informal garden design, though, for the Islamic runnel and French canal used water to link separate areas of the garden. But the fact that still water lies horizontally, serves to link a variety of features in the garden cohesively and most importantly gives the scale to the overall image.

The relationship can easily be seen at Stourhead, where the water harmonizes the tall evergreen and deciduous trees with the classical

Pink, purple and red primulas add a rich beauty to
the waterside at Longstock on a dewy morning.

buildings, which appear with ivory opalescence against the dark dense background of trees and shrubs. A feeling of movement is achieved through reflection and through the winding contours and carefully hidden boundaries of the bodies of water. Instead of a lake, the water was made to look like an imperceptibly slow-moving and broad river, evoking a mysterious languidness that was not apparent in previous water design. This languid movement is a great part of the beauty of water cities, such as Venice, Amsterdam or Suzhou in China.

ANIMATING YOUR POOL

A sense of movement can be created in various different ways. Breezes, of course, will distort the reflections and paint a mosaic of fragmented shards of colour. In England, though, planting has always been important in design and, carefully done, this will give a sense of movement to the water feature. Even a small round pool with clearly-defined borders can be animated with plants. On hazy summer afternoons, you can savour the rich growth of the waxy lily-buds, the spreading of the leaves on the water, and listen to the whispering heads of the luxuriant marginal plants. The evenings will bring out a different beauty, as insects hover over the water and the surface prickles with activity. Aquatic life will add interest to the pool, and you can spend hours watching the flickering embers of the fish dreamily voyaging through their submarine world.

In this way, either an impression of movement, or movement itself, should be carefully considered when designing your pool. Whether formal or informal, a still water feature should express this potential for movement. After all, in its natural environment, water is in a state of flux. Small fountains and water falls, brimming water, reflection, evocative contour or planting will all contribute towards animating still water.

CONTAINMENT

The method of containment is more important in the design of passive water than in active water. Containment defines the role of the water feature. In Islamic and French gardens, water is contained within a simple formal border, which differs from the naturalistic sloping waterside of the English tradition. Each approach presents water in a different way. In mediaeval and renaissance fountains, for example, the containment was considered more important than the water itself. Water filled elaborately curved basins and spouted out of the mouths of Gothic lions, gargoyles and classical motifs. In these cases the sculptural qualities of the water have

This modern treatment of the traditional *tsukubai*
is relieved by the delicacy of the bamboo pipe
that feeds it, and the careful arrangement of the
plants.

greater aesthetic impact than the actual flow of water.

When designing any water feature, an important point to consider is whether you wish the container or the water to be the focal point. A great deal depends on climate. As a general rule, an ornate container in the mediaeval or renaissance style will be suitable in a hot climate, where it emphasizes the luxury of water. Indeed every single drop is precious, trapping light and magnifying it, thereby balancing, to a degree, the size of the container. In a cooler climate, where rainfall is a regular occurrence and water is not a luxury, a single drop of water will be insignificant and the container may seem irrelevant.

ISLAMIC RESTRAINT

The detail of Islamic water features seems very simple at first glance, but on close inspection shows great sophistication. The fine lines, scalloped grooves and graceful forms are designed to enhance the quality of moving water. The carved lotus flower fountain, for example, is a beautiful, but restrained design. The edging around the pool at the Court of Myrtles is another fine example of this type of restraint. It gives a unity of purpose to the overall design and brings out a quality of architectural stillness in the water, so that it harmonizes with the solid building material around it. This relationship is repeated in the negligible difference between the water level and the paving that surrounds it.

The edging also serves to exaggerate the sense of geometric perfection in the courtyard, where a horizontal plane of water complements the vertical buildings around the pool. In this way, a precise edge confirms water as part of a formal architectural ensemble. This kind of pool should always be kept brim-full, or the solid architectural effect will be marred. The space between the edging and the water level will be doubled by its own reflection, which will make the level of water in the pond look even lower than it already is.

The border of the *parterre d'eau* at Versailles, however, raises the water above ground level, holding it up to the sky to maximize its reflection, and create an uninterrupted relationship between earth and sky. It differs from the raised Islamic pools partly in that its edge is garlanded with eight statues and partly because it is not enclosed within a courtyard. The water becomes a medium to trap light. This technique is effective in climates with the low cloud ceiling typical of northern countries.

The arc of this pool's edge, surrounded by paving,
gives the garden, the work of Japanese gardener
Inoue, an almost sculptural quality.

SPACE AND SERENITY

At Stourhead the containment of water looks completely natural. The slopes run down gently to the water, apparently without artificial intervention; the graceful contours of the shoreline cradle the peaceful waters of the lake. The gradient, which one always assumes continues at the same degree under water as above it, is most important because it indicates depth. Consequently a steep gradient would suggest a deep pool and a shallow gradient, a shallow pool. It is always worth observing this rule when designing a pool, especially an informal one. Remember that a gentle gradient will give a greater sense of space than a steep gradient because it will create less shadow. A minimum of shadow gives the water a greater surface to reflect light. In the English tradition, passive water emphasizes the shape and volume of water and should give an impression of space.

One of the most powerful impressions water can create is an atmosphere of calm and serenity. This does not necessarily depend on informal containment. In the Court of the Myrtles water takes up most of the available courtyard space, but the visitor nevertheless experiences a peaceful feeling. This ambience will depend on the depth of water, which if too shallow will look absurd, and if too deep, can become oppressive. This impression of space can be very welcome in a small town garden, where the limitations of a rectangular walled enclosure can be cleverly overcome by a simple water feature.

PRECISE LINES, RAISED POOLS AND BORDERS

Three different types of containment can be used to achieve this. The first possibility is the Islamic style, in which the water is edged by a precise line of paving. This will be effective if the water feature is to be stylistically linked to the house, so that the water becomes absorbed into the spirit of the architecture — as in the Court of Myrtles, where the water looks like a sheet of glass. Neither the paving nor shape need have a regular geometric pattern and a variety of different materials and shapes can be used. To reinforce a link with the house, however, it is best to find a compatible material and a shape that suits the style of the building.

The second possibility is a raised pool. This can be built either with man-made materials, such as brick, or with natural materials such as rough stone. My own feeling is that as it can never hope to integrate into natural surroundings like an informal pool, it should be treated formally with man-made materials. The raised pool is a perfect solution to a dark, enclosed garden because it will attract light. Such conditions, in which there

Maples and evergreens form a delightful setting
for the zig-zag bridge and stone lanterns of this
Japanese-style garden at Tatton Park, in Cheshire.

is little natural sunlight, will not be ideal for aquatic plants, so it is best to concentrate on exploiting all the reflective possibilities of the pool. Consider water as you would a mirror glinting in a dark room: it reflects what little light creeps in through the window.

An alternative form of containment is a landscaped border. Naturally, a slope and plants will require more space and light than in the previous types, and it might therefore be less suitable for a town garden. However, even if your garden is not large, you can achieve a landscaped look: either miniaturize the scale of the pool by careful plant selection, as in the Japanese style; or keep an informal shape of pool, but dispense with the slope.

REFLECTION

Reflection is one of the great joys of passive water, as sound is of active water. Water's reflective properties can be employed to achieve a wide range of effects. The magnificence of the Taj Mahal stands in contrast to the seeming veneration of the reflections in the surrounding pools. In China, the reflection of the moon in the pond is said to be the gateway to a mermaid's palace. Similarly, great importance was attached to arched bridges – since in China the circle is a symbol of heaven – and if the water level was just right, the bridge together with its reflection would appear to form a perfect circle.

Although edging is not essential to a reflected image in water, it can enhance the effect as a frame can a picture. This technique is used in many Islamic gardens, where the interplay of object and reflection produces magical results. The effect is particularly striking when the building is colourful, with intricate textual detail, as in the gardens of Isfahan, in Iran. Here the reflective action is reciprocal – often the reflection of light on the water creates a vivid shimmering on the walls of the building.

When water is placed in close proximity to a building, light will play an important part in the relationship between the two. Depending on its position, the building and the water can be lit separately by the sun. The intriguing contrast of dark water and light building, or vice versa, is often exploited by landscape designers and architects.

Consider, for example, the aesthetic impact of a dark, looming castle surrounded by the opaque rill of its moat or, in contrast, a high-tech, glinting glass building and the water in front of it like a slab of black, polished marble. This *chiaroscuro* effect will depend more on the positioning of the building than on its texture.

The sense of formal containment given by the
paved border of this pool at Faringdon House is
set off by the delightfully informal – almost
surrealist-effect of the statue.

REFLECTIONS ON YOUR POOL

Reflection is such an important aspect of still water that it is a great pity not to make the most of it. To do this you will have to consider both the positioning and size of the pool. Reflections will be most varied if the pool is sited near the house. Clouds, vegetation or a sculpture will be reflected when looking from inside the house; and when looking at the pool from the garden, the image of the house itself will be seen.

Bear in mind that height will also make a big difference. The Islamic pools were placed low because they were often viewed from a seated position. An important point to remember is that the reflection will only be effective if the base of the pool is black. A white base has quite different properties, causing the water to sparkle more, but making reflections look faded and muted.

A light-coloured finish — normally white or sky blue — is often used in municipal fountains and swimming pools, and this colouring has great artistic possibilities. David Hockney, for example, has painted wonderfully effective ripple-patterns at the bottom of a swimming pool. With the right paint and a little initiative you can make a pattern at the bottom of your water feature. As an alternative, try making a mosaic pattern with treated bricks or stones. However, light-coloured finishes have their disadvantages; nothing is more displeasing than the sight of rotting leaves and debris accumulating at the bottom of a swimming pool in autumn and winter.

Finally, remember that reflection works better if the surface of the water is free from plants. If you wish to have aquatics, they should be planted sparingly. Alternatively, opt for reeds along the border: these will stand upright, and make a pleasant contrast with the glassy reflections in a still pool.

The design of any passive water feature will depend to a large extent on climate and geography. Nevertheless, personal taste as to the form a passive water feature should take, also plays an important part in the initial design concept. By observing some of the above principles, the water garden designer will reach a greater understanding of this very versatile medium.

The skilful placing and vital shapes of the rocks
add spirit and animation to this carefully contrived
stream setting, designed by Ken Nakajima.

MOVING WATER

CASCADES AND WATERFALLS

While still water evokes a sense of serenity and space, moving water possesses altogether different qualities: vitality and life. And in the same way that reflection is a property of still water, sound is a property of moving water. Water creates a variety of sounds: the resonance of a single drop; the comforting murmur of a stream; or the splash of falling water. There is music for every mood.

The Moghuls were the pioneers of the formal use of large quantities of moving water, building wide cascades in their gardens in Kashmir. Through skilful design, the raw material was transformed into effervescent white sheets and fine mists of spray, from which all the colours of the rainbow unfolded. Designers have made great use of the refractive and reflective properties of the surface of water, changing light in the same way as a prism. When illuminated by direct sunlight, the effervescence of a foaming white cascade can produce a superb effect. The *chadar* cascade in Kashmir is an example of this art at the peak of its perfection; there is a magical fusion of water, energy, air, sound and light.

The *chadar* is a veil of water laid on marble carved into a thousand scalloped shells or prisms. The water courses down the marble slope, churned up and aerated by tiny air pockets until it looks like a white crystalline sheet. The Sicilian poet Ibn Hamdis described it in rapturous terms in 1132: "Waters are like ingots of silver which meet on the steps of the *Shadirwan*".

When building a waterfall, a variety of techniques can be utilized to create unusual effects. Velocity is important, as is the edge over which the water falls. Curling edges, for example, will create a curtain-like cascade. If the edge is crenellated, the water will be divided into separate jets. At Chatsworth, in Derbyshire, at least five different kinds of lip create different falls of water. In Kashmir, the Moghuls again demonstrated their aesthetic skills in their treatment of transparent sheets of water; they carved niches, called *chinikinas*, into the wall behind a curtain of water. At night candles

The black rocks and frothing water of this superb
Nakajima design, at Matsushima in Japan, leave a
lasting impression of raw power and movement.

flickered in the niches and during the day the candles were replaced by golden vases planted with silver flowers. This idea should be easily within the grasp of the amateur designer and with careful planning, should make an original and successful water feature.

In Italy, moving water was seen as a joyful expression of vitality and life. The Italians' sense of freedom and fun was borne out by countless tricks and gimmicks involving water. One amusing and eye-catching water feature is the *ovato* at the Villa d'Este, designed by Ligoria. Drawing on the idea of the water curtain in the Moghul garden, the *ovato* is essentially a semi-circular waterfall behind which people can walk and experience the wonderful sensation of looking at the world through glistening sheets of water. The scale of this trick makes it difficult for the amateur to achieve the effect, but it is not impossible.

THE NATURAL WATERFALL

It was the power of the natural waterfall that inspired the American architect Frank Lloyd Wright. His masterly, *Falling Water* is a house designed to project over a natural waterfall. The unceasing flow of water unifies the house with its natural environment, so that it becomes a harmonious part of the surrounding rock strata and foliage. Dappled by the play of light, *Falling Water* is a prime example of how water can be used to bridge the gap between architectural design and natural form.

Waterfalls similarly inspired American designer Lawrence Halprin, whose major works include the Auditorium Forecourt Fountain and the Lovejoy Plaza in Portland, Oregon. Both are immense theatres of water, expressing the essential ruggedness and brutality of water in a thoroughly modernistic way: water gushes and streams in cascades and waterfalls from the top terraces to a pool.

In Japan, however, moving water is treated in a more reserved fashion. The main aim behind a Japanese waterfall is that it should imitate and idealize nature and not appear artificial. In the Japanese vocabulary a number of metaphorical terms describe the different characteristics of waterfalls: *nuno-ochi* is a white cloth hanging down; *ito-ochi* is a screen of thread; a s*ayu-ochi* means falling from right to left; and a *kasane-ochi*, falling in two or three stages.

Although the desired effect was one of informality, Japanese garden designers were always aware of a number of constraints. Like all features in the Japanese garden, the design of a waterfall conformed to a set of rules. Sometimes, as in the Sanzon Ishigumi, the waterfall symbolized the unity of

The sparkle and energy of this simple fountain by
Geoffrey Collins, in Munich, stands in contrast to
the natural stone and sharp lines of the building.

three figures in Buddhist belief. Alternatively, the reference was to a natural phenomenon: the pointed rock at the foot of a waterfall, for example, which hints at the vibrant form of a leaping carp.

FOUNTAINS

The fountain adds another dimension to moving water. Unlike the waterfall, the fountain is rarely a natural phenomenon, but the fact that it is man-made means that more often than not it becomes the focal point of the composition. Buildings, open spaces and garden foliage are put in perspective by a fountain, so that however many disparate elements are featured in a landscape design, the overall effect will be one of visual unity.

Until the 20th century, the fountain played an important role in society. It marked the centrepoint in towns and villages, where people could gather to exchange local gossip and collect water; but the siege of our squares by hectic traffic and the installation of municipal water supplies have both contributed to its demise. As a result, the aesthetic principles behind fountain design no longer have to be tempered by practical concerns.

But, ironically, it has recently been discovered that the fountain is beneficial to the physiological and psychological health of city dwellers. Water falling in the form of rain, waterfalls and fountains generates a negative static charge — or ionization — that attracts positively charged particles such as carbon dioxide. These particles, which are thought to have a depressant effect, are concentrated in urban areas. The running water of a fountain catches the particles in the water and deposits them in a filter system. So perhaps the civic fountain will take on a new lease of life.

FOUNTAINS AS SYMBOLS AND IN RELIGION

There are many different types of fountain, but one particularly interesting example is the Japanese *tsukubai*. This usually takes the form of a round stone basin of clear water. The basin is constantly replenished by water, which drips slowly but regularly from a length of bamboo pipe. The *tsukubai* has both a symbolic and a functional place in the Japanese garden; on the one hand it represents purity and simplicity; on the other, the water is scooped up with a bamboo ladle to cleanse the hands before the tea ceremony.

Islamic fountain design is similarly restrained, as the fountain serves a religious purpose and is mainly used for ritual ablutions before prayer. Unlike the *tsukubai*, however, which blends harmoniously into the garden composition, the Islamic fountain is designed to stand out against its

Set against light plumes of pampas grass, the
dancing streams of water in this superb pool
becomes an intrinsic part of Carl Miller's
sculptures.

surroundings, a refreshing contrast to the heat and dust of a hot climate. The water is often forced upwards through a central spout: this is different again from Oriental custom, in which water normally flows downwards.

THE FOUNTAIN AS ART

The European fountains of the Renaissance were pieces of sculpture in their own right. Some of the best examples can be found at the Villa d'Este, in Italy, where, among many choreographic uses of water and many fountains sculpted in human form, there stands a remarkable sculpture of Diane of the Ephesians offering a bountiful supply of water through her multiple breasts. The Trevi fountain in Rome, built in 1762 by Salvi, is a fine example of Baroque sculpture. Its fluid lines give the illusion of movement and the statues are animated by the luminosity, vitality and sound of water.

The idea of using water to express light, movement and sound in sculpture was interpreted in a very different way in the Constructivist movement at the beginning of the century. In it, moving water represented space. The pioneer of Constructivist art, Naum Gabo, believed that the emphasis in art should be on space rather than mass. In his revolving sculpture at St. Thomas's Hospital, in London, Gabo represents the space occupied by a three-dimensional circle through the interplay of light and water. By changing its spatial relationship to its surroundings, it becomes dissociated from volume and mass.

But perhaps the most compelling characteristic of a fountain is its fascinating cyclical transformation. The water is expelled under great pressure upwards into the air before spraying outwards and falling in showers. As it falls, a powdery spray of tiny drops is framed for a second, before shattering the water surface. This process continuously repeats itself: the crystalline column; the dancing plume; the feathery mist — all change the character of the water surface from a flat, passive mirror to a vibrant, active plane.

Today, modern technology has added a new dimension to what was already a multi-dimensional form. Different nozzles can be used to create a myriad of complex spray patterns, and time clocks and electronic controls can be used to change sets of nozzles and choreograph a kaleidoscopic splendour of effects. But it is important that one is not too distracted by these tricks: water design in the past has been successful mainly because it has had a spiritual and contemplative purpose underlying a visual attraction.

Delicate sprays of water give a feeling of
weightlessness to Naum Gabo's revolving
sculpture by the Thames at St Thomas's Hospital,
London.

THE WATER GARDEN TRADITION

Stourhead, in Avon, laid out by the Hoare family in
the mid-18th century, spearheaded the
development of the English landscape tradition.

PERSIA

ETERNAL OASIS TO PARADISE GARDEN

The history of the water garden can be traced back to the cradle of civilization: to the bare rock, scorched earth and denuding winds of Mesopotamia, some 3,000 years before Christ.

Mesopotamia was a hostile, barren land, but lying between the Rivers *Euphrates* and *Tigris* it had the potential to be fertile — if only water could be channelled and controlled to irrigate the land. So long as this could be done, life was sustainable; if the irrigation systems broke down, the agricultural soil would crumble back to its dusty origins.

So water was a vital life-force to primitive man: a necessity that demanded respect. Such dependence led, inevitably, to a philosophical interpretation of water's place in the scheme of things, and even a religious veneration for its use and qualities. The water garden developed as an expression of early man's reverence for water and his respect for its powers. It stood as a symbol of a very practical Paradise: for the Mesopotamian desert-dwellers this meant an eternal oasis, with abundant fresh water and exotic, lush foliage. Without water, there could be no garden, and no life, so water was emphasized as the central part of every garden, demonstrating each builder's temporal resources and spiritual concerns.

BABYLON

For several thousand years, Mesopotamia was a shifting sand of prosperous city states, fabled empires, conquering kings and pillaging, nomadic tribesmen. This very flux both helped develop the resources to build gardens, and spread the techniques and impetus for creating them.

The aggressive proto-Indo-Europeans, for example — once known as 'Aryans', until Hitler abused the term — introduced the concept of the water garden to Persia at the beginning of the first millennium BC. King Nebuchadnezzar, celebrating the rebirth of the once-proud Babylonian Empire around 600BC, built the Hanging Gardens of Babylon to remind his wife, a Median princess, Semiramis of her homeland. Tiered and terraced,

Built around 2,000 years after the Hanging
Gardens of Babylon, Fatehpur Sikri, near Agra, in
India, still retains the feeling of an eternal oasis in
a sandswept desert.

with rich green plants glistening with water in the heat of the Middle Eastern sun, they were one of the Seven Wonders of the ancient world.

Unfortunately, all of these early examples of the water gardener's art are lost to us, buried under the parched dust that they temporarily held at bay. But the ruins of one ancient garden survive, giving us an opportunity to speculate about their original form: Pasargardae. According to Xenophon, the Greek mercenary and historian, writing in 401 BC, Pasargadae, near Isfahan in modern-day Iran, was planted personally by Cyrus the Great, the founder of the Persian Empire, in 546 BC. The design takes the form of a rectangular court, bounded by two palaces and two pavilions, enclosing a walled garden. (In old Persian this was called a *pairidaeza*, a term from which the English word "paradise" was derived.) A shaded colonade surrounds each pavilion, providing a cool recess ideal for relaxation and quiet contemplation of the silver gleam of water in its tight runnels and the colourful, fragrant flowers that the Persians loved so much. This idea was subsequently developed into the *talar,* or columned porch, used as the point of contact between garden and house, with one projecting into the other — an important concept in later garden design.

Sometime after *Pasargardae,* a design of singular importance came to be incorporated into the traditional *pairdiaeza* form. It is called the *Chahar Bagh,* a form that can be seen from *Mesopotamian* ceramics some 6,000 years ago to Islamic garden design of the present day.

Essentially, the *Chahar Bagh* design consists of a cross, symbolizing the division of the world into four sections, with the pool of life at its centre. The four sections can be interpreted, variously, as the four elements: fire, air, water and earth; and as water, milk, honey and wine. The *Chahar Bagh* thus becomes a symbol or order, emphasizing harmony and interdependence.

The precise date this quadripartite form came to be applied to garden design is not known, but it was certainly by the 2nd century AD. Worked in silk, gold and precious jewels, the Spring Carpet of *Khusrau II* depicts an abstract perspective of central watercourses, plots of flowers and birds of many different colours.

There is one main variation of the *Chahar Bagh*. Sometimes, the water at the centre of the design was replaced by a pavilion — as at Hasht Behist in Isfahan, Iran — where water channels led away from the surrounding buildings and towards a central fountain (this centripetal effect is perhaps most evident in the Patio de los Leones at the Alhambra in Spain).

The intricate detail of the Mosque at Isfahan, in
Iran, is beautifully reflected in the brimming pool.

THE RISE OF ISLAM

It was perhaps the artistic sensibility that came with the idea of quiet contemplation that enabled the spirit of Persian garden art to survive the conquering inroads of other civilizations — that of Macedon, for example, led by Alexander the Great in 324BC, and of Rome, in the 1st century BC — with extraordinary resilience. The Arabs who invaded Persia in 641AD also gradually became converts to Persian culture.

The Arabs found a highly-developed garden art based on the three precepts: the *Chahar Bagh*, the pavilion and the veneration for water. But to these precepts had been added a sense of aesthetic sensibility — an appreciation of exotic plants, architecture and materials — that derived from Persia's geographical position at the mercantile crossroads between Asia and Europe. Persia's native plants, for example, such as vines, jasmine, saffron and onion, had been augmented by a huge number of new varieties that had travelled the silk and spice routes from the East. In all respects, Persia had become one of the most highly developed nations of the ancient world.

But the Arabs did recognize certain elements of the world they had conquered. The Persian garden, for example, represented a tangible image of the paradise described in the Koran: the fertile "garden beneath which rivers flow", with its "spreading shade", "fruits and fountains" and "cool pavilions". And it was the juxtaposition of the tangible Persian concepts, of the *Chahar Bagh* and pavilion, with the non-specific images in the Koran that gave rise to the Islamic Paradise garden. This became the essential art form of the Arabs, from southern Spain to north-west India.

The focus of the Islamic garden was water, used as a reference to, and as an expression of, abstract qualities. This is a key difference to the use of water in other garden traditions, in which water is used in the form of a lake, waterfall or river — in other words in a realistic way, with specific connotations of nature.

For the Arabs there was no connection with nature. Water was celebrated for its own properties: in a fountain and basin, for example, its vertical movement is contrasted with its horizontal stillness; in a straight narrow channel, or in a brimming pool, there would be a sense of water's solid, yet ephemeral nature; and on a *shadirwan*, a carved marble slab, later developed into the *chadar* used in India, water was expressed as a delicate film or veil.

The Islamic water garden found perhaps its
highest form of expression in Spain, as here in the
Patio de la Acequia, in Granada.

SPAIN

THE ISLAMIC GARDEN

I n 711AD, the North African Moors invaded Spain. It was the beginning of an occupation that was to last more than 750 years; a conquest that flooded the stagnation of thought in Europe's Dark Ages with the light of Muslim science and knowledge.

Part of this fund of wisdom — all of it new to Europe — was philosophical; part was horticultural; and part, of hard necessity, was practical. The Moors brought to Spain a reverence for water as a generative force and an appreciation of simplicity — even minimalism — in its use; and also a love of plants and flowers.

Horticulturally speaking, the Moors imported numerous exotic trees and plants that had originated in the Far East and been adapted to more temperate climates: lemons from Asia, for example; citrus fruits from India and Japan; oranges from India; and a variety of flowers and spices. Finally, and most importantly, for the water gardener, the Moors brought with them sophisticated techniques for the management of water.

CORDOBA AND GRANADA

Cordoba, in the plain of the River Guadalquivir, was the Moors' administrative capital, and demonstrates these techniques in action. The plain was watered by a network of small canals, all drawing on underground reservoirs. One Cordoban garden — the *Patio de Los Naranjos* — demonstrates clearly the cross-over between the practical irrigational skill of the Moors and their appreciation of clean, simple lines. It consists of an orchard of orange trees, each linked at its base to a geometrically arranged network of narrow water channels, fed from the overflow of a reservoir.

But the showpieces of Moorish garden design are to be found not in Cordoba but in Granada. Some 30 miles (50k) north and west of the Mediterranean, Granada enjoys a unique blend of tropical and mountain climates. Five rivers supply an abundance of water, giving the Moors far greater opportunities for using water than at Cordoba.

An extravagant tunnel of water in the *Patio de la
Acequia*, in the Generalife at Granada

Granada is dominated by the Alhambra, the fortress-palace of the 13th-and 14th-century Moorish kings of Spain. Also known as the Red Castle, it is made of a deep rust-coloured material called ochre, which acquires a different, vivid tinge according to the time of day. The effect of these sultry reddish tones against the azure-blue sky of the late afternoon is unforgettable. So, too, is the artifice with which the inner sanctuaries, set in a parched desert-scape, are made to seem brimming with water.

THE COURTS OF THE ALHAMBRA

Granada boasts a number of spectacular examples of the Islamic garden. Perhaps the liveliest, but least characteristic, of these is in the Generalife, which was built in the mid-13th century, before the Alhambra, and used to house the ladies of the court. The main focus of this complex is the *Patio de la Acequia*, or Court of the Long Pond — on entering it, one's first impression is of a tunnel of water. In fact, the illusion is formed by plumes of water that spurt upwards from either side of a 55-yard (50m) pond: in such burning heat, this represents sheer abandonment. On either side of the pond are borders of flowers and hedges, while circular fountains representing lotus flowers occupy its centre and ends.

The Alhambra is separated from the Generalife, which lies higher up the hill, only by a dividing valley. But the water gardens in the Alhambra appear austere in contrast to the vigour and excess of the *Patio de la Acequia*. The *Patio del Mexuar*, for example, in the Mexuar Palace just by the Alhambra's entrance, consists of a small court with a lotus-shaped fountain at its centre. The use of water is restrained here, as distinct from the lavish use of decoration on the opposite wall.

The *Patio de los Arrayanes*, or Court of the Myrtles, said to have been built by King Yusuf I, who died in 1354, is different again. A superb artistic composition, it has a very practical function — the breeze that blows across its water provides a surprisingly efficient air-conditioning system for the palace. The Court is rectangular — 47 yards (43m) long by 25 yards (23m) wide — and encloses a large pond set in marble pavement and bordered by paths and clipped myrtle hedges. The texture, colour and shape of these plain hedges and paths is set off by the fine stonework of an elegant colonnade, called the *Torre de Comares*, opposite. But perhaps the most inspired feature of this Court is that the surface of the water is almost level with the marble paving. There is a mere hair-line between the building and its reflection, which appears almost unearthly.

The latest of the famous water gardens to be built in the Alhambra was

The fluid architecture of the Court of the Myrtles,
in the Alhambra, is reflected in the easy grace of
its fountains and pool.

the *Patio de los Leones*, or Court of the Lions, started in 1377. A highly decorated low gallery, supported by 124 white marble pillars, encloses a courtyard some 40 yards (35m) long and 5 yards (4.5m) wide, into which jut cloistered pavilions at either end. The whole courtyard is a controlled riot of colour, with blue, yellow and gold decorations on the walls and different shades of paving tiles. At the centre is an alabaster basin, supported by 12 stone lions, known as the Fountain of the Lions.

The handling of water within the courtyard is very successful in terms of unifying the design and in giving a deeply sensual impression of water. From each side of the Fountain flows a narrow water channel, interrupted at intervals by small, circular pools. These channels, which refer back to the Persian *Chahar Bagh* concept, are used to interesting technical effect, for they link the diverse parts of the design physically and give meaning to the variety of shapes, textures and colours. As a result, they have a strange effect: they seem to make the buildings part of, and subordinate to, the fountain complex, rather than the other way round.

Our sensual appreciation of the water is heightened by the simultaneous movement of water in the Fountain and in the channels. As the Arab poet, Ibn Zamrak, describes it:

"Silver melting which flows between jewels, one like the other in beauty, white in purity; A running stream evokes the illusion of a solid substance for the eyes, so that we wonder which is fluid."

A MONUMENT TO THE MOORISH TRADITION

The Alhambra stands as a shining monument to the Moorish branch of the Islamic tradition – in fact, it represents the artistic high-point of the development of the water garden until the tradition was taken a step further in the Moghul gardens of 16th-century India.

At its heart, this branch of the tradition was rooted in the vision of a desert oasis, replenished by life-giving, utilitarian water. But, in Europe at least, the Islamic tradition of water gardens was to come to a dead end. In 1492, the Moors were forced back to North Africa by Ferdinand and Isabella of Spain, locking the doors behind them and keeping the keys – many of which still exist today – in the hope of eventual return. But this was not the only reason why the Islamic tradition had little potential for development in Europe: the European climate, too, militated against Islamic design. After all, the delicate plume of water from an Islamic fountain can never fully satisfy the sense if it is blurred by sheets of rain.

Ornate Stucco work, supported by a family of
pillars, encloses a shaded fragment of the palm-
tree oasis in the Alhambra's Court of the Lions.

INDIA

THE MOGHUL GARDEN

In 1218 Genghis Khan swept across the central Asian steppes with a horde of mounted bowmen and established the Mongol Empire. With Khanates in Russia, China, Persia and India, travel, communication and security were guaranteed. Around 180 years later, in 1398, Timur the Lame, the Mongol Ruler of Samarkand – the subject of Christopher Marlowe's famous play, Tamburlaine the Great – set out on another round of conquest, of Persia, Russia and India. Timur was completely ruthless and his invasions were likened at the time to a plague of locusts. Yet, paradoxically, Timur was one of the great gardeners of history. He sent the Persian water gardeners back to Samarkand, which quickly filled with Paradise gardens.

In Samarkand, the geometric plans of the Persians and their characteristic use of water were modified by Mongol practicality. The result was the *Gul Bagh*, or rose garden, in which a new kind of vitality was breathed into the spartan contemplative plots of Persian gardens. They came to be cluttered with traditional nomadic tents, for example, and were used for grand festivities. Restraint in the use of water became less important as the canals gradually became wider, and the sound of water began to play its part. The whole style started to mirror the difference between Persian sophistication and Mongol earthiness.

THE TIGER'S GARDENS

As a young boy, at the end of the 14th century, a descendant of Timur called Babur, or 'Tiger,' conquered Samarkand, and no doubt saw the water gardens at Court. Within a few years, in 1504, he was to become the first Moghul Emperor and later follow in the footsteps of Alexander the Great, by invading India.

Initially, though, Babur did not take to India. Babur's followers disliked the place so much that they pleaded with him to return home. Fortunately, though – for the sake of water gardens at least – Babur was not to be

The bridge in the causeway at Lake Dal, in
Kashmir, set against a mysterious backcloth of
distant, snow-capped mountains.

persuaded. For like his predecessor, Timur, Babur was a great gardener. In Persia, he had more or less followed the traditional Persian concept of *Chahar Bagh*, building a series of gardens along the bank of the River *Jumna*. Enclosed and divided into four parts they were, but the water channels were treated differently, being considerably wider, and much less numerous, than in the original *Chahar Bagh* design.

But Babur found a very different world on the other side of the River *Indus*. Unlike the arid platforms of his homeland, the gentle hills of Hindustan were covered with lush and exotic vegetation. The Persian tradition of enclosure and of clear, regimented axes was incompatible with the climatic conditions and topography. It was also not a tradition with which the local inhabitants would have felt in sympathy, for the Indians of Hindustan had never had any fear of drought — after all, major irrigation projects were not needed, since the massive rivers of the *Indus* and *Ganges*, guaranteed a constant, year-round water supply.

Their temperament lacked a sense of discipline in the use of water, and they had never found it necessary to impose such symmetry as had the Persians on their interpretation of nature. Hindustani buildings, for example, were dark, mysterious and secret, contrasting sharply with the thought-out, clear-cut and open quality of the Persians, for whom indeterminate shadows could only mean danger. Water was revered by the Indians, but for reasons of religion, not of scarcity: the lotus flower, with its roots anchored in the mud, but its flower high above the surface of the water, stood as a metaphor for human aspirations.

So as the Moghul garden developed — effectively, it was the Eastern branch of the Islamic tradition — it subtly melded three influences: the austere, clean-cut Persian water garden; the lustier, more practical input of the Mongols; and the more undisciplined approach of the Hindustanis.

MOGHUL GARDENS

Most of the Moghul gardens that survive were built by Shah Jahan, the fifth Moghul Emperor, during the first half of the 17th century. The exception is the garden at *Shalimar Bagh* — it means 'abode of love' in Sanskrit — on the shores of Lake Dal, in Kashmir. Still thought of today as a true representation of Paradise, *Shalimar Bagh* was created by Shah Jahan's father, Jahangir, whose reputation as a garden designer exceeds even that of his son.

In Jahangir's time *Shalimar Bagh* would have been reached by boat. The visitor crossed the lake and travelled up a long, lily-laden waterway

A celebration of marble and water, Shah Jahan's
Taj Mahal rises majestically behind a glassy
watercourse.

bordered with poplars, being drawn inexorably into the geometry of the garden's design.

The garden consists of three terraces, bisected by a long canal and adorned with cascades. This form inspired many later designs — probably even those of the Villas D'Este and Lante in Italy. The lowest terrace was used for receiving guests, and is dominated by the imposing facade of the *Diwan-i-Am*, or Hall of Public Audience, through which the 7-yard (6m) canal flows. Jahangir would have sat within this Hall, looking out over the arrivals. His *chabutra*, or throne, was a rectangular slab of black marble, sitting in the centre of the canal and reached by steps. Decorated with an ornate painted ceiling, the *Diwan-i-Am* must have dazzled the visitor, as streaks of light reflected from the water set off the decoration and lit up the Emperor's clothes.

The second terrace is separated from the final terrace by a spectacular effect: a three-sided cascade masks a series of carved niches, called *chinikanas*. During the daytime, these would be filled with gold vases and flowers; during the night, with candles. The cascading water would be lit up by the candles, giving a delightful translucent effect, described by the 19th-century traveller and writer the Vicomte Robert d'Humières as a "sheet of mobile crystal".

The final terrace contains the famous Black Pavilion, named for its columns of black marble. The Pavilion, called a *baradari*, which means 'twelve doors', is really a large summerhouse, from which one can watch the water cascading through the garden. The Pavilion is surrounded by water, and can only be approached across an arcaded causeway; in fact, the Pavilion is obscured by a mist of spray thrown up by fountains, making it truly a world of water. Vicomte d'Humiéres describes the scene perfectly, in *Through Isle and Empire*, written in 1905:

"Four other rows of spouting fountains in the basin itself raised, as it were, a forest of silver lances around the kiosk with its glittering marbles. We were surrounded by the splashing, by the efficient coolness of the heavenly water, the glory of the consoling water, the feast and the apotheosis of water."

Jahangir's gardens at Lake Dal primarily demonstrate the Moghuls break with the Persian tradition in the way in which the landscape is used as a part of the design. *Shalimar Bagh's* whole atmosphere depends on the dramatic shape of the silhouetted mountains and the pure water of the lake. The

The epic scale of the Taj Mahal is relieved by
harmony of its proportions and its essential
simplicity.

Black Pavilion becomes the meeting point between the mountains and the lake, and give the impression that it is the source of the water. As a result the garden celebrates nature in a way that is clearly incompatible with the Islamic emphasis on the properties of water itself, and the exclusion of nature as a design consideration.

THE TAJ MAHAL

Jahangir may have broken with the Persian tradition, but his son, Shah Jahan, returned to the classically Persian *Chahar Bagh* for his most famous work: the Taj Mahal.

Shah Jahan started work on the Taj Mahal in 1632, intending it as a mausoleum for his wife, Mumtaz Mahal. The material he chose was marble, and it is this that gives the building its special appeal. Marble has a particular quality that can never be constrained, even when it has been carved: depending on the light, it subtly changes, like a crystal spectrum; it shimmers defiantly in the noon-day sun, yet glows seductively in the twilight. And the varying moods of marble are enhanced by water, an element that the Taj Mahal celebrates equally.

Like Jahangir, Shah Jahan placed his building at the end of a long watercourse, impelling the visitor towards it. The watercourse is much wider than a traditional Persian one would have been, and is made to appear wider still by the use of black and white marble ripple paving, which simulates water. (A similar technique was used at the *Shalimar* Garden at Lahore, though in this case the material was brick.) The Taj Mahal itself sits on a plinth, which symbolizes a rectangular pool, and makes the building look as if it is floating. This impression is reinforced by the reflections of the marble in the water when the Taj Mahal is viewed from the other side of the river. Shah Jahan's whole design is intended to express the concept of purity transcending life.

But the Taj Mahal illustrates Shah Jahan's skill in his use of water in other ways, too. A *purs* system drives water through the garden: buckets of water from the River Jumna were carried up to a storage tank by fairly unsophisticated means: teams of oxen hauled them up a ramp. The system itself, however, is more highly developed: operating on three levels, it demonstrates how a tyrant can satisfy almost any obsession if he or she disregards its cost in physical labour.

THE FORT AT LAHORE

The capital of the Punjab in modern-day Pakistan, Lahore was once one of

The graceful platform and bridge on the middle
terrace of Lahore's *Shalimar* Garden give a false
impression of the potential power of its fountains.

the most important cities of the Moghul Empire. It first became so when Emperor Akbar, the third Moghul, built a fort there, and its position was reinforced when Shah Jahan started to construct the Royal Road of Mauryan, which linked Lahore with Agra and Delhi. In 1642, he started to build what is today the best-preserved of all the Moghul gardens: the *Shalimar Bagh* of Lahore, about a day's march from the fortress.

Like Jahangir's *Shalimar* on Lake Dal, the garden at Lahore consists of three terraces, bisected by a canal, of which the highest terrace was reserved for the Emperor and his family. At the end of the Emperor's terrace, a pavilion spans the canal and gives a commanding view of the whole garden. Sitting at his *chabutra*, Shah Jahan would have been able to see a truly magical sight: water coursing down a magnificent marble *chadar* behind his throne and flowing into a large, rectangular pool. Shah Jahan's *chabutra* was evidently a development of his father's *chabutra* at Lake Dal, being surrounded by rails on which to lean one's elbows.

The marble *chadar*, a sculpted and decorated slope behind the throne, would have framed and flattered the silhouette of the Emperor against a crystalline sheet of water. He, meanwhile, would have been enjoying the steady, murmuring whisper of the water as it flowed round him, and been soothed by its cooling properties. The rectangular pool itself, much larger than in previously constructed gardens, is divided into two parts by a central platform, reached on each side by a bridge. Standing on short pillars, these bridges almost seem to hang on the surface of the water; they are devoid of any detail, balconies or carvings, so people walking across them would have either been reflected in the water, or half-seen as hazy figures in the mist and spray of the hundreds of fountains in the pool itself.

This effect is ingenious enough, but so, too, is the *Jawan Bhadun* cascade on the final terrace. Here, the water is lit up by candles at night-time and flowers during the day, in the same way as in Jahangir's *Shalimar Bagh* at Lake Dal, before flowing beneath a marble walkway. But today Shah Jahan's Garden at Lahore, though still beautiful, retains only a fragment of its former glory. Much of the agate and marble decoration was stripped away in the 18th century and used in the building of the *Ram Bagh* at Amritsar.

A columned pavilion gives a cool, shady view of
Lahore's *chadar* and *chabutra*.

ITALY

THE WESTERN TRADITION STARTS

T hough the first water gardens to be built in Italy owed much to Eastern influences and to culture and religion of ancient Greece, subsequent designs came to embody the philosophy and religion of the Romans.

Hadrian's Villa at Tivoli, built between 118 and 138AD, is a good example of a classical Roman garden, from a time when the power of Rome was at its height. It consists of a large collection of buildings erected almost haphazardly, each of which acted as a reminder of a building or site that Hadrian had seen during his travels. The most significant of these is the Canopus, based on the temple – now in ruins – to Serapis, a Greco-Egyptian god, on the Nile delta near Alexandria.

Hadrian dug out a valley to construct the Tivoli garden, making an open space 130 yards (119m) long and 20 yards (18m) wide. Half of this area is filled with an expanse of water called the Canopus canal, which is flanked on each side by colonnades and statues. Hadrian's guests would have entered the area along a striking semi-circular arcade at one end of the canal, and feasted in the *triclinium*, or dining room, at its far end. This was an apse-like structure, later copied in the Oval Fountain at the Villa d'Este. Dinner at Tivoli must have been a magical experience: the walls would have glittered with a film of water, which when it reached the floor would have spread outwards like the probing ripples of the rising tide to fill small canals that surrounded the reclining guests, replete with their stuffed dormice and peacock's tongues. It must have seemed to the diners that they were drifting free on the canal in a boat, amid the ghostly reflections of statues of the gods.

THE RENAISSANCE

Hadrian's Villa at Tivoli is perhaps the best of the surviving classical Roman gardens, but it did not mark the start of continuing trend in garden design: from the fall of the Roman Empire to the Renaissance, garden art was

Guests at Hadrian's Villa at Tivoli would walk to
dinner along this striking arcade to the dining
room at the other end of the canal.

almost confined to the growing of vegetables.

It was not until Boccaccio, the father of the novel, and Petrarch, the poet, had heralded the Renaissance with their colourful descriptions of nature in the mid-14th century that garden design began to flower once more. Petrarch's measure may be judged by the fact that he astounded his contemporaries, to whom such an idea was bizarre, by climbing a mountain purely in order to appreciate the view. His writing makes it clear that he believed in recapturing the spirit of classicism, and also that he saw the garden as the ideal place for meditation and thought.

A century later, in 1452, the Florentine, Alberti (1404 – 72) wrote a treatise to Pope Nicholas V. Called *De Re Aedificatoria*, this laid down the principles of Italian garden design for years to come. With thought balanced by action and mind by heart, Alberti was the emblem of the "complete man", of the Renaissance. He often quoted the "practice of the ancients" – in fact, many of his ideas were taken from the gardens of the younger Pliny and the writings of Vitruvius.

Alberti's treatise was written at a time when the aesthetic undercurrents civilized world were changing direction: the Byzantine Empire ended with the fall of Constantinople to the Turks in 1453; Moghul art had reached its zenith with the building of the Taj Mahal; and China and Japan were going through periods of relative artistic sterility. As a result, Italy and Renaissance Europe had become the standard-bearers for creative forces, and they were able to draw on a wealth of scholarship and influences.

But perhaps the main impetus for the Renaissance was the sacking of Rome in 1527. This brought about an acceleration in the evolution of intellectual values, with acceptance of an idea that became fundamental to the Renaissance: that man was centre of the universe. This led to a concept of individuality. Applied to garden design, it ultimately freed the garden from the house, giving it an identity of its own.

THE VILLA D'ESTE

Just two miles from Hadrian's Villa at Tivoli, the Villa d'Este is a prime example of the development of this concept put into practice. Built in 1575, it has a nearly limitless supply of water: 264 gallons (1,200l) per second, carried by aqueduct from the River *Aniene*. Not surprisingly, therefore, water is the inspiration and theme of the garden. It is not used in the Islamic way, however – far from it. At the Villa d'Este, there is no sense of water being functional, and being treated with reverence: it is used with technical brilliance to delight and surprise the visitor; and the surprises are often

A riot of cascading, jetting water gives this corner
of Hadrian's water garden at Tivoli a sense of
exhilaration.

earthy and indelicate.

From the old entrance on the Tivoli road, the visitor is first struck by a series of terraces, which draws the eye up to the grand villa. This treatment has an unexpected historical precedent in, among other Moghul gardens, Jahangir's *Shalimar* garden in Kashmir and strongly suggests that Renaissance garden design in Italy was rooted in Islamic principles. On each terrace, water is treated in a different way. The Pathway of the One Hundred Fountains, for example, consists of three rows of fountains – the effect is of an army of vertical and horizontal silver plumes.

In some respects, the Villa d'Este resembled a Renaissance Disneyland. *Automatae*, or mechanical devices powered by water, were a feature of the garden. They included an organ that generated a famous trumpet call; a dragon that produced sounds of cannon shot and musket-fire; and an owl that intermittently stopped the steady chirp of birds perched on bronze branches with an eerie hoot. There were even thoroughly frivolous *Giochi d'Acqua*, or practical jokes played with water: the seats at a lunch party might suddenly erupt with water, for example.

But this extravagance and inexhaustible vitality in the use of water, coupled with its sheer abundance, comes to a head in the garden's statue of the goddess Diana of the Ephesians. In a metaphor repeated throughout the garden, water spouts from her breasts, in a symbol of jubilant eroticism and fertility. Here, as in the garden as a whole, the visitor is committed, not to reverence as in the Islamic garden, but to pleasure.

THE VILLA LANTE

Designed by Vignoble in 1564, the Villa Lante is also a masterpiece of 16th-century garden art. Most significantly it represents an important stage in the release of the garden from its domination by the house. Instead of overlooking the garden, the house is cleverly built into two parts, on either side of the main axis of the garden's design. Beside the Villa d'Este, though, Lante is quiet and unassertive. In fact its whole atmosphere is one of sensitivity and grace – especially in Vignoble's interpretation of the garden as a part of Nature.

On entering, the visitor sees a magnificent statue of Pegasus, the winged horse of myth, by Giambologna, prancing with muscular energy in a shaded pool surrounded by nymphs. Pegasus is the guardian of the Bosco, or hunting ground. The garden itself is made up of several shallow terraces – another reference to the Islamic design that utilized varying levels. The lowest one is square, equipped with a central fountain that was originally

The vertical and horizontal plumes of The Pathway
of 100 Fountains, at the Villa d'Este.

surrounded by flower *parterres*, or low, ornamental designs made from box shrubs. The fountain sits in a pool divided into four parts by bridges, in a form reminiscent of the Persian *Chahar Bagh*, and in each pool miniature muskets and trumpets discharge water at the fountain.

The second terrace is really a garden dining room, with a stone table containing a water channel, designed to cool wine, at its centre. From here, the *parterre* garden and lake and the "purple distance" described by Sir George Sitwell can be seen framed by specially planted trees. Continuing up the terracing, plants follow the course of a *cordonata*, or chain cascade, at the end of which the Dolphin fountain, bathed in a sun-lit space, throws out delicate, sparkling plumes of water.

THE MOST FAMOUS FOUNTAIN IN EUROPE

Some two hundred years after the Villa Lante was built, in 1762, architect Niccolo Salvi blended classical references and naturalistic effects in the most remarkable way, in the *Fontanda de Trevi*. It is undoubtedly the most spectacular fountain of the 18th century, and probably the most famous fountain in Europe.

Salvi used the mythical importance of purity in water to provide an iconography for the fountain, making it a complete representation of water: of its benevolence and its unpredictable qualities. This double-sided nature was crystallized by John Bullein in his *Bulwark Against All Sickness*, in 1562: "Water is a good servant, but it is a cruel master".

But in Greek myth, all forms of water had to submit to its master, Oceanus. *Oceanus* was a great river that flowed in a circle around the earth; from the river, they derived the name of Oceanus, the god of all water – as opposed to Neptune, who rules over the seas alone. At Trevi, therefore, the central figure of Oceanus, around 19 feet (5.8m) high, holds a sceptre, rather than a trident. Standing on an oyster shell, he is flanked by two tritons, each with a horse. The horses stand for the two faces of water: one is raging and tempestuous; the other is calm and placid.

The overall effect of the design is rather like that of a theatre, in which the audience congregates in a semi-circular recess that curves round the structure. On the stage, it seems as if the rough, semi-crystalline rock formation is a billowing wave about to crash down into the auditorium, with awesome figures of myth surging with the water in a frenzy of sound and fury.

The jagged crags of travertine seem to be still
forming in Rome's Fon tana de Trevi, almost
overpowering the triton and his horse.

FRANCE

THE INSPIRATION OF THE SUN KING

Although there are no surviving examples of mediaeval gardens, it seems likely from later representations and the buildings that remain that the mediaeval garden was much the same all over Europe, apart, that is, from minor variations in the plants grown — mainly in the area of fruit trees and herbs. It can be summarized as having an internal courtyard containing a limited variety of plants. Some gardens — especially monastic ones — also used water in a purely functional way: the stewpond, in effect a larder for fish.

Over the years, this most simple of garden forms evolved into the "knot garden", consisting of an intricate arrangement of the plants within a square, and it is from this that the French garden — and in particular, the geometric *parterre* garden — developed.

And so matters stood — until, that is, Charles VIII's invasion of Italy in 1495, and the writings of French travellers, such as Montaigne, brought the influences and new thoughts of the Italian Renaissance to France. French intellectuals welcomed the idea, first bruited by the Roman philosopher Vitruvius at the time of Christ, that beauty was a harmony of all parts; this had been developed by Alberti, who formulated the purist concept of beauty in perfect proportion. Consequently, a pure classical and architectural model emerged. The claustrophobic superstition that had paralysed mediaeval man and indoctrinated him with a fear of Nature's dark forces evaporated, and this idea of pure design provided him with proof of man's superior intellect.

But there were great differences in topography and climate between Italy and France: the wide flat acres of Northern France had little in common with Italian slopes and terracing. Flat, marshy conditions meant that there was always a need to control water, for drainage and irrigation, while water could rarely be forced through fountains or at sufficient pressure to create a permanent head. As a result, ornamental canals, rather than fountains and waterfalls, came to be characteristic of French garden design.

During mediaeval times, water was essential for defence, but even when

Parterres – designs created by an intricate
arrangement of plants within a border – were
features of the French tradition, as seen here at
Versailles.

this became unnecessary, buildings such as the Palace at Fontainebleau and the Chateau at Chantilly were built near water – partly, no doubt, through a paranoic fear of wide open spaces, and partly because it was so difficult to construct systems to carry water. When the Italian influence demanded the presence of elaborate cascades and fountains, even though these were not really native to France, elaborate and ingenious mechanisms had to be devised – as, for example, at Versailles.

VERSAILLES AND THE *MACHINE DE MARLY*

The impetus for the construction of Versailles came, of all things, from a party. Louis XIV, the all-powerful Sun King, attended a party given by his finance minister, Nicholas Fouquet, at the impressive Vaux le Vicomte. Louis felt himself eclipsed by the splendour of Fouquet's garden; as a result, and with breath-taking arrogance, he imprisoned Fouquet and employed the best designers available to build Versailles and demonstrate his superiority over his nobles: Le Vaux, the architect, Le Brun, the painter and interior designer, and le Nôtre. Though it was a collective effort, Andre le Nôtre takes much of the credit for the marvel of Versailles, though the final word, of course, belonged, to the ever-fastidious Louis.

The site for the garden of Versailles was a small traditional garden inherited from Louis XIII. It was bounded by a vast swamp and monotonous country, and the first task was to provide a supply of water. The problem was solved by the construction of the extraordinary *Machine de Marly*, a system of 14 large wheels that helped draw water from the Seine; in its time it was one of the wonders of the world.

The design for the gardens is based on a long, east-facing axis cut by several transverse lines. The axis starts from the building's facade and is bounded on either side by symmetrically planted tress. Victor Tapie, in *Baroque et Classicisme*, published in 1972, talks of "the whole logical progression from the design in stone to the open countryside". Indeed, "logical" is the key word. It is a design based not on seducing the viewer with sensuous curves and unexpected twists, but on an instant revelation that satisfied both the intellect and Louis' materialistic and conceited nature. The design might well have been influenced by the current vogue for theatre, in which the curtains are raised to reveal an unknown, artificial world.

But not everything is visible at first sight, and Louis himself wrote a day-long itinerary that afforded spectacular views as one walked from one fountain to the next. Although the treatment of the garden is ostentatious

Elegant and proud, the Vaux de Vicomte stands
mirrored in one of its many water features.

and arrogant, it is nonetheless magnificent – especially when one considers the surrounding terrain and the scale of the project, and sees how perfectly Nature has been moulded to satisfy an obsessive hunger.

But, most significantly, the design marks the spirit of discovery. The use of water, for example, shows an understanding of dioptrics – the theory that states that the angle of reflection is equal to the angle of incidence – in the way in which water is placed to reflect the facade of a building. The axial design, in turn, shows the discovery of linear perspective, also used in the theatre, to give an illusion of depth. At Versailles, the ideas of modest compartmentalized gardens were swept aside and replaced by a fearless application of these new techniques.

The Palace of Versailles itself is built on a low hill from which avenues radiate with perfect symmetry, like rays from the sun – Louis' own emblem. In fact, the sun is a highly significant metaphor in Versailles and provides the iconography of the entire layout. According to the royal historian Félibien, the sun motifs are linked to Apollo:

"It is proper to point out that, since the Sun is the King's device and since poets identify the sun with Apollo, there is nothing in this superb edifice which is not linked to this divinity."

The Apollo sun-god allegory is expressed in many parts of the garden. The Latona fountain, for example, is named after Apollo's mother; in the *Grotte de Thétis*, destroyed in 1648, Apollo was refreshed by fawning nymphs after his exertions – though scarcely naturalistic, the grotto is said to have contained elaborate ornaments made from rock and shells and various hydraulic effects, including a water organ.

From the huge entrance gates, the visitor is taken across an intimidating expanse of cobbles, before reaching shelter in the Palace. The park is on the other side of the palace; its steps offer an uninhibited view across several epic water features.

The first of these are the splendid water *parterres* on either side of the central axis. These rectangular pools reflect both the reclining statues that personify the eight main rivers of France and the graceful horizontal lines of the palace – but, most of all, they reflect light, trapping it in the same way as a mirror does in a darkened room. Even on a misty, lugubrious day, the diffused light creates an indefinable but uniform white blankness on the water. The effect is such that the way in which water was contained at Versailles gave a stylistic lead to the future use of water in the cloudy

The majestic plant and water *parterres* of Vaux le
Vicomte, stretching away into the French
countryside.

northern countries.

The Latona fountain, though, with its tiered base, grotesque creatures and statue, cannot be seen until the end of the first terrace is reached, since the garden is on a gradient. The fountain is circular, and on a smaller scale than the other water features. It consists of three raised basins, positioned in concentric rings, with stairways curving around to give a sense of shelter and enclosure. By placing the whole system in such a position, the designer has created a self-contained space, distinct from the dominion of the palace.

Following the central axis down the grassy *Allée Royale*, the next water feature is the magnificent Apollo fountain, which shoots up, on rare occasions, a column of water 80 feet (24m) high – an *Obelisque d'Eau*. This fountain is superb: figures of muscular horses surround Apollo, their furious hooves as if to thrash the water and create an eruption in the centre of a pool surrounded by tall trees and reflecting mysterious arching avenues. Although far from pastoral, one cannot help comparing it to Giambologna's statue of Pegasus at the Villa Lante.

Versailles has had so many water features – including 1,400 fountains, though not many remain – that it is impossible to describe each one. The east-facing, tree-lined canal, however, is worthy of comment. Wide, long and traversed further up by another canal, it was the scene for a variety of entertainments: they included trips in a frigate, and jaunts in two sumptuous gondolas operated by genuine Venetian sailors. The canal is, perhaps, at its best in the twilight, when the setting sun glows red at its end, lighting up each water feature along the axis with the colour of burnished copper.

Today it is impossible to fully appreciate the glory that was Versailles, because there is little moving water. Even in its heyday, Louis' progress through the garden was carefully monitored so that underlings could synchronize the turning off of one fountain and the turning on of the next. Now the water is only turned on for certain days during the year, and the garden's discipline and order remains generally unrelieved by the poetry of its fountains.

The magnificent facade of Versailles, reflected in
the water placed by Andre le Notre to create this
effect.

ENGLAND

THE LANDSCAPE TRADITION

T he landscape school of garden design, for which England was to become famous, started as a reaction to the conceits of the fashionable French style. That is not to say, however, that the French garden was never accepted. In fact, in 1689, The Tudor Palace of Hampton Court boasted an elaborate *parterre de broderie* – an arrangement of ornamental box hedges so complex that it resembled embroidery – designed by Daniel Marot, a pupil of Le Nôtre's. *Parterres*, hedges, allées, canals, fountains and bosquets – ornamental groves intersected by paths – were all copied from France, and retained their popularity right through the reign of William and Mary. At Chatsworth the outline of the formal plan can still be seen today.

But in 1710 the formal style was attacked by Anthony Ashley Cooper, the 3rd Earl of Shaftesbury, in an article in the *Moralist*. He advocated "things of a natural kind: where neither Art, nor the Conceit or Caprice of Man has spoil'd their genuine order .... Even the rude Rocks, the mossy Caverns, the irregular unwrought Grottos and broken Falls of Water with all the horrid graces of the Wilderness itself, as representing Nature more, will be the more engaging and appear with a magnificence beyond the mockery of princely gardens."

In 1712, the essayist Joseph Addison followed up this attack, writing in the *Spectator*: "The Chinese laugh at the plantations of our Europeans, which are laid out by the rule and line, because they say anyone can place trees in equal rows and uniform figures. They choose rather to discover the genius in trees and in nature and therefore always conceal their art." Alexander Pope, one of the greatest poets of the 18th century, was the next to join the fray. He attacked the monstrous artificiality of current gardens, appealing to his readers to follow nature and to bring out the *genius loci*, the spirit of the place.

Whether it was the inherent romanticism of the British that was responsible, or the influence of new ideas, filtered back from the Far East

A mediaeval-style stew pond at Newstead Abbey,
in Nottinghamshire, is complemented by a tree-
lined avenue of water that stretches into the
distance.

by Jesuit priests, it was clear that the philosophy of garden design was undergoing a revolution. It is also true that this revolution was both inspired and reflected by the work of the new painters: men such as Nicholas Poussin and Claude Lorraine, from France, and the Italian, Salvator Rosa.

THE TRANSITION

Naturally, these new ideas were not put into practice straight away. There was a transition period, and one of its leading figures was Charles Bridgeman — perhaps the first great British garden designer, who died in 1738. Bridgeman collaborated with the architect John Vanbrugh at Stowe, among other places, and together they had an enormous influence on the development of the new art of landscape.

Bridgeman is credited with the first use in Britain of the ha ha — a sunken ditch that prevented cattle from crossing over into the garden. It was a kind of waterless moat that did not interrupt the view and allowed park to merge imperceptibly with lawn. The vital importance of the ha ha, in the words of the writer Horace Walpole, in 1771, was that it "set the garden free from its prim regularity, that it might assort with the wilder country without." So the garden came to be seen as more than an extension of the house: in fact, as an expression of Nature; while the house became an architectural feature within Nature.

But it was left to William Kent (1685 – 1748) to finally break away from any lingering attachment to the rigid, formal design that had so conditioned his predecessors, and, in doing so, to become the first professional English landscape gardener. Kent's style probably derived not only from his observations while travelling in Italy, but from an appreciation of the Claudian — that is, following Claude Lorraine — style of landscape painting.

Kent's work developed these influences in an imaginative and enterprising way. It drew on two main techniques: first, his trick of providing sculptural features, such as miniature Greek or Roman temples, either at resting places or as focal points, in a way that was subordinate to the overall unity of the design; second, his treatment of water, as described exuberantly by Horace Walpole:

"But of all the beauties he added to this beautiful country, none surpassed his management of water. *Adieu* to canals, circular basins and cascades tumbling down marble steps, that last absurd magnificence of Italian and French villas. The gentle stream was taught to serpentine seemingly at its

An embodiment of autumnal calm at the lakeside
at Stourhead.

pleasure, and where discontinued by different levels its course appeared to be concealed by thickets properly interspersed, and glittered away at a distance where it might be supposed naturally to arrive."

In essence, Kent's contribution to the genre was to give a sense of intimacy to an art-form that had always previously aspired to the heroic.

STOURHEAD

Though designed by Henry Hoare, a banker and amateur gardener, Stourhead, in Avon, is nevertheless a splendid example of the new principles put into practice. The project was begun in 1740, and completed some 30 years later by Hoare's son.

Stourhead is a lake landscape, smaller but more unified than the similar idyllic Claudian landscape at Vanbrugh's Castle Howard, in Yorkshire. The garden is quite separate from the house, the only point of connection between the two being an obelisk — for the idyllic garden, this is part of the outside world; by the same token, it lends the house an air of unreality and mysticism. Apart from the presence of this single reminder, the design and function of both house and garden is self-contained.

The garden is designed round a three-lobed lake, fed by a river, whose boundaries are never made clear. This gives the garden the appearance of being much bigger than it is. The lake is enclosed by splendid trees and carefully contoured slopes, often — and controversially — disguised today by dense clumps of rhododendrons. The one side that is open, and which presumably dammed the river, delineates a contrastingly sharp and obviously man-made arc.

The shores of the lake are punctuated by classical buildings: a Palladian bridge, a grotto and a more recent Gothic church. A path follows the shore and offers the visitor seductive glimpses of these remote and graceful buildings across an expanse of water. The stroll was designed above all to be an aesthetic experience, a retreat into the world of classical antiquity.

It is thought that Hoare used the Roman poet Virgil's epic work, the *Aeneid*, as a source, since the classical allusions reflect Aeneas's wanderings after the fall of Troy and his descent into the underworld at Lake Avernus. The allegorical journey starts at the Temple of Flora and follows the lake to the grotto. This is a wonderful surprise, with a rugged stone arch and a lugubrious dampness that contrasts vividly with the light, clinical elegance of the classical buildings. In the darkness, a luminous white river god beckons one into a domed chamber, lit by an opening in the centre of the

Neo-classicism blends with a spectrum of colours
reflected on the lake at Stourhead.

dome. On the left, a small, rustic opening in the rock gives a view of the lake, though the writer Joseph Spence, in 1765, tells us that it was originally equipped with a curtain. In a stony recess on the right, running with water, lies a Sleeping Beauty, bathed in diffused light, while water pours from the beckoning river god's urn, as if to form Stourhead's lake.

The allegorical journey continues as the visitor reaches a temple called the Pantheon of Earthly Glories, which houses, among others, a statue of Hercules. It is completed by a walk through a rocky arch to the Temple of Apollo, perched on top of a small hill as if a symbol of the world of the gods, to dominate the lake below.

CAPABILITY BROWN

William Kent died in 1748, to be succeeded by an even more famous English gardener: Lancelot, nick-named "Capability", Brown (1716 – 83). Unlike Kent, who was more of a landscape designer than a landscape gardener, Brown had a wide-ranging knowledge of plants – acquired during his days as director of the main gardens at Stowe – and this gave him greater confidence in their use.

Within a few years of Kent's death, the Claudian garden landscape started to lose its popularity. This was primarily because an unthinking juxtaposition of different architectural features in gardens resulted in a displeasing lack of unity. Also, while Gothic ruins and wild grottos may have represented the culture of northern Europe, they hardly suited the English landscape. The logical solution appeared to be a smoothing and emptying of the landscape. Brown adopted this solution whole-heartedly, and spent his creative life drastically re-arranging his predecessor's gardens - even though he sometimes attracted a great deal of criticism.

Capability Brown's style is perhaps seen at its best at Blenheim Palace. Blenheim was a gift from a grateful nation to the British General, the Duke of Marlborough, to mark his victory over the French and Bavarians at the Battle of Blenheim, in 1704. Originally the garden had consisted of *parterres* and a majestic bridge built by Vanbrugh that spanned the narrow, canalized River *Glyme*. Brown's approach was, to say the least, drastic. He tore out the *parterres* and replaced them with the lawn that now runs right up to the house – this sweep of lawn, devoid of any architectural line, and the abrupt appearance of a building, is characteristic of Brown's work.

Next, he dammed the *Glyme* and formed twin lakes that were connected by Vanbrugh's bridge, itself much reduced in size by the increase in the water level. Again, the use of a lake is characteristic of Brown's work. The

Delicate fountains power a superb formal cascade
at Chatsworth, in Derbyshire.

final feature of a typical Brownian landscape is the use of clumps and belts of trees. These are planted in strategic locations, with great attention being paid to the effects of light and shade. The belts hug the contours, undulating with them, having the twin effects of ensuring a sense of intimacy, and, as a result of the interplay with perspectives, creating a depth and variety in the landscape.

But the greatest achievement at Blenheim goes beyond this confident handling of lawn, water and trees. It lies in the skilful sculpting of the landscape in a way that strikes a deep chord: a primeval quality of abstraction and sensuality. Brown's sensitive handling of form and contour became the distinctive stamp of the English landscape garden, and established its identity. In the words of Horace Walpole:

"We have discovered the point of perfection. We have given the true model of gardening to the world. Let other countries mimic or corrupt our taste, but let it reign here on its verdant throne original by its elegant simplicity, and proud of no other art than that of softening Nature's harshness and copying her graceful touch."

CHATSWORTH

Chatsworth, in Derbyshire, the historic seat of the Dukes of Devonshire, is an unlikely setting for one of the most splendid water gardens in Britain. But from the modest approach road, the imposing facade of the building hides a multitude of water features: canals, cascades, fountains and even jokes, powered by hydraulics. These technical triumphs stand in magnificent contrast to the drama of the landscape, in a way that would be unimaginable in a formal environment.

The presence of these water features is due to Chatsworth's unique supply of water, which runs off the moors to be contained in a huge lake that powers the entire garden. The energy produced is substantial: when the garden is closed to the public today, the flow of 3,000 gallons (13,680l) per minute is used to generate electricity. The changing fashions of each era, as Chatsworth was remodelled by successive Dukes of Devonshire, manipulated and developed this potential, with the result that, today, the garden is an amalgam of many different styles.

Chatsworth was first laid out between 1687 and 1706 by George London and Henry Wise, the last of the English formalists, who had together worked at Castle Howard and Longleat House, in Wiltshire. At Chatsworth, irrespective of the natural contours, they carved a formal

Paxton's Emperor Fountain at Chatsworth shoots
an impressive jet: it is one of the highest naturally
powered fountains in the world.

design of terraces, *parterres* and fountains on to a steep slope. In 1694, though, Grillet, a pupil of Andre Le Nôtre, laid out a cascade above these terraces — it has since been widened — making up the axis of the garden. The water that feeds this cascade comes from the "Temple", a small semi-circular building that arches round a pool which is constantly replenished by water from a variety of elaborate fountains. The novelist Daniel Defoe described the scene in 1724:

"Out of the mouths of beasts, pipes, urns, etc., a whole river descends the slope of a hill a quarter of a mile in length, over steps, with a terrible noise, and broken appearance."

The design of the cascade is a considerable technical achievement. It consists of a series of steps, each a different distance from the preceding one, and a different height. Each step, too, is a different shape, changing the appearance and the sound of the water: sometimes it falls in a clear sheet, for example, and sometimes in a white spray.

One of Chatsworth's jokes also dates from this time: in 1692, a willow tree was constructed from copper, whose branches hide jest of water that can be turned on to drench unsuspecting visitors.

In the 1760s, Capability Brown destroyed the formal terraces and replaced them with 3 acres (12,000sq m) of lawn, known as the "Great Slope"; he also planted belts of trees and diverted the River Derwent so that it flowed away from the house. Fortunately, though, Grillet's cascade survived these modifications. But the last major change — and the final style to be employed to Chatsworth's gardens was the responsibility of Sir John Paxton (1803 – 65), who became head gardener in 1826.

Paxton built the Great Conservatory, the predecessor to the larger structure at Crystal Palace, to house the exotic plants sought out by the Victorians. It needed an enormous amount of coal to keep it at the correct temperature, and fell into disrepair after the First World War — but not before, it is said, it had housed the first banana to ripen in England. However, Paxton's Emperor Fountain still works perfectly. Situated in the Canal Pond, on the axis of the house, it shot up a jet of water around 87 yards (80m) high, making it the highest naturally powered fountain in the world.

In a confident expression of Romanticism, Paxton also constructed the magnificent ruined aquaduct with its dramatic waterfall, which looms beyond the Temple as if it was free-standing. Again, Paxton placed huge boulders, collected from glacial deposits, in immense rockeries such as the Wellington Rock, to evoke a monstrous and marvellous primeval world.

17th-century joke, Chatsworth's copper willow
tree is seen here in action, ready to soak the
unwary visitor.

CHINA

AN APERTURE TO THE WORLD

Addison may well have been correct when he wrote, in 1712, that "the Chinese laugh at our European plantations", for by then China was able to draw on a long tradition of water gardening, and to a philosophy for the creation and appreciation of beauty that was already nearly 8,000 years old. The tradition arose, in part perhaps, as a result of China's resources in terms of wealth and labour; but the main reason for it was undoubtedly the country's legendary, even fantastic, landscape.

Long before Petrarch, Chinese scenery had been eulogized in literature and painting. In fact, the word "landscape" is translated in Chinese as *shanshui*, meaning hills and water. This interpretation is integral to Chinese culture and philosophy, and especially so to the design of a garden. Guilin, in the Guangxi province of south western China, gives us one example of this link between landscape, literature and philosophy. A famous beauty spot, it is surrounded by mysterious-looking limestone hills that are shaped like teeth; in Chinese poetry these are compared to green lotus buds, shooting up from a jade green river.

Another example is Huang Shan, one of the many religious mountains of China, south-east of Shanghai. Famous since the Tang Dynasty 1,200 years ago, the mountains of Huang Shan comprise 72 peaks, the highest one being called Lianhua Feng, or lotus flower peak. A tortuous stairway carved into the rock leads to the peaks; pine trees cling on to the mountains, brushed by wispy clouds and contorted by the wind. Between the rock spires, people trickle past each other like ants on a tree trunk. The sheer height and the barren, wild seclusion of Huang Shan is a powerful image, and one that is often described in verse, as here by the poet Li Bai:

"Huang Shan is hundreds of thousands of feet high, With numerous soaring peaks lotus-like, Rock pillars shooting up to kiss Empyrean roses like so many lilies grown amid a sea of gold."

A 17-arch bridge spans Kuming Lake at Peking's
Summer Palace Gardens, adding a perfectly
contrived design feature to the natural landscape.

But the Chinese contrasted their reverence for mountains with an equal, but different, reverence for water. The twin principles became the foundations for the concepts of Yin and Yang, the two elements that fuse the world. As Confucius put it:

"The wise man delights in water, the good man delights in mountains. For the wise move but the good stay still. The wise are happy, but the good secure."

Yin is a female principle, embodied by passivity, darkness, water and the moon. Yang is a male principle, represented by vitality, assertion, sun and mountains. The garden – a microcosm of the world – contained the essence of these qualities, and so symbolized a healthy balance between Yin and Yang, and harmony with cosmic forces. Consciousness of these forces is basic to Chinese thinking, so much so that they were formalized into a metaphysical system called Taoism. In the 6th century BC its doctrines were embodied in a book called *Laotzu*, which taught people a life of superior virtue, based on submitting oneself to cosmic forces and becoming one with nature, a practice called *Yang Hsin*. Artifice of any kind was rejected and the virtue of nature was extolled – particularly the virtue of water. As *Laotzu* says:

"There is nothing softer and weaker than water and yet there is nothing better for attacking hard and strong things."

THE MYSTIC ISLES OF THE IMMORTALS

The Chinese garden had its roots deep in this philosophy, since it provided a rare opportunity in a city for a person to become one with Nature. And one particular reference that was always uppermost of the minds of Chinese garden designers was to the myth of the *Hsien*, or Immortals. These lived on mystic isles off the East coast of China, and were carried about by gold cranes. Successive Chinese emperors spent lifetimes in obsessive attempts to discover the secrets of immortality – they believed, for example, that the water that seeped from stalactites might be the elixir of eternal life, so searched mountains for them – and dedicated their gardens to symbols of their searches.

But immortality, according to ancient Chinese legend, meant "eternal life beneath the waves". As a result, grottos were often a feature of Chinese gardens, built beside lakes and streams. Rocks, meanwhile, represented the

Maples and pines interweave with the elegant
structures to enhance the idyllic waterscape of
Wang Shih Yuan at Souchow.

islands, while gazelles, tortoises, storks, goldfish and exotic plants both symbolized an exotic paradise and, supposedly, encouraged the Immortals to linger and bless the occupants with longevity and prosperity.

So the Chinese garden tradition, completely unlike that of Europe, rests on a complex base of symbolism and philosophy, containing references to landscape, the principles of Yin and Yang, Taoism and the myth of the Immortals. Yet the Chinese garden itself was made up of hills, rocks, and water arranged with a curious mixture of an eye for contemplation and for vivid chaos, for the sentimental and the grotesque.

HANGCHOW AND SOUCHOW

Although seriously damaged by T'ai-ping rebels in the 1860s, Hsi-Hu, the West lake of Hangchow, is still a good example of Chinese garden art. On the southern margin of the *Yangtze* delta, this silver lake rimmed by blue mountains is said to have attracted a community of Buddhists as early as 200AD. During the later Sung Dynasty (1127 – 1280), it was the site of China's Imperial capital: a contemporary proverb said, "There is heaven above and Souchow and Hangchow below".

In this period, Hangchow's prosperity, based on the trade brought by the Grand Canal that linked it to Peking, was legendary. For one festival the entire park was garlanded with flags, while Marco Polo, who visited the city in the 13th century, wrote that it offered "more refreshment and delectation than any other experience on earth".

The West Lake is a sequence of landscape designs, many of which have literary associations. Graceful bridges and causeways of weeping willows divide up its two-mile (3k) diameter, while its banks are studded with pavilions and temples. In the centre of the lake, a small island encloses a lake and causeways of its own.

Close to Hangchow, Souchow contains a number of good examples of another form of water garden, and one that conforms more to the Western idea of a Chinese garden. Souchow has flourished since Sung times, but most of the gardens were built during the later Ming period (1368 – 1644). The reasons for their construction are not clear, one theory being that they were a reaction against the stern disciplines of the preceding Yuan dynasty of Mongol rulers. But the theme for them all is one of effete ornamentation.

The garden of Wang Shih Yuan – the Garden of the Master of the Fishing Nets, and reputedly the work of a disillusioned bureaucrat – is one such garden. Romantically hidden behind idiosyncratic crenellated walls, it is no more than an acre (4,000sq m) in size – tiny, considering the generous use

Natural stone and native plants help give Wang
Shih Yuan's buildings the appearance of floating
on water.

of water and the busy arrangement around it.

The garden and the buildings form a tiny outpost of watery seclusion, with the buildings, connected by covered walkways, very much part of the design as they often are in Chinese gardens, but never seeming to encroach. Instead, they are subordinated to the beauty of the rocks and water, for they serve only as vantage points from which to appreciate the garden's beauty. Outwardly, the buildings consist mainly of white walls, with elegant vermilion wooden supports, grey tiles, exquisite lacquer tracery and carved windows.

The acute contrast between the undisguised workmanship of the structures and the crudeness of the rocks often surprises Westerners. But the discrepancy is explained by the 18th-century writer, Shen Fu:

"In laying out garden pavilions and towers, suites of rooms and covered walkways, piling up rocks into mountains, or planting flowers to form a desired shape, the aim is to see the small in the large, to see the large in the small, to see the real in the illusory and to see the illusory in the real."

The buildings are about three feet (0.9m) higher than the water, and look down on the peaceful world they surround. Rocks and water alone are represented, with little space for plants – though a number of trees fan the water's surface, giving the garden freshness and a touch of colour. In a western garden, a lawn would probably be substituted for the water. But this idea would have seemed ridiculous to the Chinese, as Tung Chu-In explained in 1936: "While no doubt pleasing to a cow, a lawn could hardly engage the intellect of human beings".

It is clear that the Chinese gardeners looked for something that could never be provided by a lawn: the sense of exhilaration and space lent to a scene by an expanse of water. The western writer William Chambers, in his *Dissertation on Oriental Gardening*, published in 1757, captures the concept perfectly, saying that a clear lake is like:

"A rich piece of painting, upon which the circumambient objects are represented in the highest perfection; and the Chinese say, it is like an aperture in the world, through which you can see another world, another sun and other skies".

An ancient Chinese treatise on garden design, called the *Yuan Yen*, confirms this view:

"The mirror of the pond reflects the shadows; here is opened an entrance to the mermaid's palace".

The Zhouzheng garden, at Souchow, with a raised
walkway from which visitors can reflect on the life
of the pond, and the "entrance to the mermaid's
palace".

JAPAN

A UNIQUE PERCEPTION OF NATURE

From the time that Japanese culture and European culture first made contact, in the 17th century, the relationship between the two has been fraught with misunderstanding. Few Westerners have paused to try to understand the unique perception of life that has emerged from Japan's rich and complex tradition. And — more than in most cultures — the Japanese garden stands as a symbol of the country's view of man's relationship to life and his concept of beauty.

Japanese culture — like that of China — stresses a deep bond with Nature that is difficult for Westerners to appreciate. The bond is based on a rhythm of life, with changes of season and climate having major significance to everyday life. Each new season is carefully defined and celebrated: the progress of the cherry blossom, as it flowers in different areas at different times, is something of great interest and delight; when autumn lights up the trees, it is welcomed like a long-lost friend, and crowds gather at beauty spots.

In the West, by contrast, the idea that Nature can only bring out our worst characteristics and that it is separate and apart from our lives has, to an extent, been taught by the Christian Church and encouraged by the glorification of the individual during the Renaissance. In Japan, such an idea is anathema. Even the landscape supports this view: scalloped shorelines, with tiny islands drifting off them; the deep blue sea; the mountains, covering more than three-quarters of the country; deep valleys, with forested hills and terraced ricefields — all predispose the Japanese to their uniquely personal relationship with Nature.

SHINTO AND CHINA

The first main influence on Japanese garden design was Shinto, a polytheistic belief in the gods of Nature that endows natural phenomena with spirits. One common expression of Shintoism was to tie a sacred straw rope around a rock or a tree as a sign of respect for the spirit that inhabited

Nature idealized: wooded islands basking in
tranquil waters at *Saiho-ji*, in Kyoto, Japan, retain
an air of 14th-century mysticism.

it. Thus decorated, the rock or tree became a shrine to the gods, and soon it would be surrounded with a well-swept area of gravel, to define it and separate it from the forest. It was now known as a *Jinsha*, a shrine, or a *Niwa*, a garden.

So, in effect, Nature itself was the object of worship and the place for such worship became what we call a garden. Unlike the western tradition, in which the garden is used to separate the house from the wilds, the Japanese tradition became that of using the garden to link man to the gods of Nature. So the Japanese house is intimately connected with the garden – in fact, in the oldest gardens the house is a graceful and fragile building that seems almost to rise up from a lake.

The second main influence on Japanese garden design came rather later: in the first century AD, when the Japanese established a colony on the Korean peninsula. From this time, Japan imported many ideas from China. It is thought, for example, that as many as 100,000 Koreans and Manchurians were resident in Japan by 600AD. They certainly had a profound influence: the city of Kyoto is laid out according to the sacred Chinese science of *shijin-so*, or geomancy.

Kyoto was to become the capital of Japan. Today, it is known as the "City of Purple Hills and Crystal Streams", and its abundant rivers and great natural beauty make it a perfect site from which to trace the development of the Japanese water garden – born from Shinto, taught by China, and finally growing into the highly developed art form that it is today.

The earliest gardens of Kyoto were built by aristocrats of the Heian family, who held sway between 898 and 1185. Usually consisting of a large pond containing three or four small islands, they were much influenced by the Chinese tradition, as a treatise on garden making by Gokyogoku Yoshitsune, called the *Sakuteiki,* shows:

"In a landscape garden, earth represents the Emperor, the water his subjects. Water flows wherever earth allows it and when earth obstructs, the water will stop flowing. It is also said that the mountain represents the Emperor and water his subjects, with the rocks as vassals supporting the Emperor. Water flows as willed by the mountains but when the mountain is weak, the water will destroy the mountain".

So the Heian gardens represent the social structure of the community. Typically, the gardens have three main components: mountain, water and rocks; each gives a meaning to the others. As in China – and in Persia, too –

A thick carpet of moss runs down to the lakeside
at Kyoto's *Saiho-ji*, 600 years ago the setting for
boating parties.

both mountains and water are powerful symbols, used in the garden on the one hand as a microcosm of the natural world, and on the other to balance the opposing forces of Nature. This emphasis in the Heian gardens clearly show the influence of Chinese Taoism: the mountain, assertive, hard and uncompromising is Yang, the intellectual force; it is balanced by Yin, the softness of water, associated with feeling.

But another feature of the Chinese garden had also taken its place in the Japanese tradition. In 219BC, Ch'u Fu, a Chinese envoy, landed at Kumano, in Kii Province. Ch'u Fu had sailed many years before, under the orders of the Chinese Emperor Shih Huang Ti, and had been told to find the three Isles of the Immortals and the elixir of life.

Ch'u Fu told the Japanese the myth of the Isles of the Immortals, and they soon assimilated it. By mid-Heian times, *Horaisan* (*Horai* was the name of one of the three mythical islands) was represented a rock in each garden's lake as a guarantee of prosperity. A line of stones in the water stood for the *Yo Domari*, or night mooring stones, suggesting a line of boats sailing towards the Isles of the Immortals.

Later, the island was to become an important feature in the Japanese garden, though not always as a representation of *Horai*. Sometimes, it stands for *Shumisen* – another island, but this time from Buddhist belief, which was credited with being the central pillar that supports the heavens. Often, too, the island was often given the shape of a turtle or a crane. The turtle, traditionally believed to live for 10,000 years, was a female symbol; while the crane, with its 1,000-year life-span, was a male symbol: both, therefore stand for longevity.

THE EARTHLY PARADISE AND THE FORCE OF NATURE

After the Heian period, new ideas began to take root in Japan. One of them was Esoteric Buddhism, whose practitioners looked for a tangible earthly paradise. Such a concept was quite alien to Shinto, in which the rhythms and cycles of Nature were held to be paramount. Nevertheless, Esoteric Buddhism was to play its part in the development of Japanese water garden design, influenced by such ideas as *Enri Odo* – the seeking of paradise – and *Gongu Jodo*, an escape from this detestable world.

The garden at Byodo-in represents just such a paradise and contains many of the symbols of Esoteric Buddhism. As is typical with such gardens, the building looks out over a lotus pond. Called *Hochi-E*, or the treasure pond, this represents one part of paradise. The Land of the Paradise Amida – the Esoteric Buddha – however, is represented by an island in the pond,

The wooden terrace jutting over this fertile and
picturesque Japanese garden symbolizes a desire
to live in close harmony with nature.

and a bridge leading to it, called *Guzei*, stands for the route that the blessed take to salvation. The building itself represents a phoenix, the symbol of rebirth, in flight, with its upturned roofs resembling giant wings. In it is a statue of the Amida Buddha, gazing calmly out across the paradise.

But these Chinese influences were not to last for long. The design of Saiho-ji, a garden in Kyoto built in the first part of the 14th century, represents a complete break with Buddhism and China. In fact, it was the precursor to the final form of the Japanese garden. The garden is divided into two parts: a flat, lower garden recalls the earlier Heian gardens, but has a new emphasis on leisure activities, such as boating; while a new barren and stony region, called Mount Koin, is a symbolic mountain. The garden's designer, Muso Soseki (1275 – 1351), justified this new emphasis on leisure in his book *Muchu Mondo*:

"It is a delusion to think that the pure world of paradise and the profane world of the present are different. The distinction between holy purity and defilement too is a delusion. Both are only groundless imaginings that spring into the human mind."

In Saiho-ji, Soseki tried to demonstrate this by showing the emptiness of an earthly paradise. The lower area represents the Land of Amida as pure but superficial – a world of tranquillity that nobles visited to admire the cherry blossom and compose poems. Mount Koin cannot be seen from this comfortable world, but once the stairs have been climbed and one has passed through the Kojo Gate, its brooding presence, casts an unforgettable shadow over both mind and body. Strewn with hard, real boulders, it is a complete contrast to the Land of Amida. So, too, is the dry waterfall, which can be seen from the Shito-an pavilion: huge granite boulders suggest the awesome strength of driving water, creating a cacophony of noise and energy in the mind.

From the time of Saiho-Ji, the Japanese garden returned to the traditional Shinto idealization of nature. Water, in particular, was appreciated, with its every aspect expressing the sensibility of nature: tranquil, smoothly contoured expanses; sinuous streams cutting through undulating hills; the remoteness and harmony of a wooded island basking in its solitude – the vitality and variety of water was now supremely important.

The gardens of Kinkaku-ji, one of the most popular tourist attractions in Kyoto, are a good example of this idealization of nature, even though

The old meets the new in this idyllic garden by
Japanese designer Araki. Water from an ancient
stone well laps at the foundation stones of a glass
and wood house.

Buddhist references are still present. Whatever the season, the eye is first drawn to the pavilion, with its dazzling golden facade: in the early winter sun its shimmering image stands remote and pure amid the snow-capped pines; in the autumn, surrounded by blazing maples, it is perfectly reflected in the water.

The lake is divided into a two areas, representing an inner and an outer sea, by a long island and a peninsula. This arrangement gives a false impression of its size, as one can see the opposite shore between the peninsula and the island. The inner sea contains five islands – one, with a symbolic peak jutting out only a foot (0.3m) from the water, represents *Shumisen*; others symbolize the turtle and the crane.

By contrast, the long island in the centre of the lake with its meticulously sculpted pine trees has been created for purely aesthetic reasons, to shelter the peace of the inner sea. Pines and water are often used together, though, both in landscape and in painting: pines represent eternity; water stands for transience.

THE ZEN GARDEN

The final element in the development of the Japanese water garden tradition – and one that, above all, gave the Japanese garden its unique character – was Zen Buddhism. Zen swept away the carved statues and visions of paradise of the preceding garden philosophies and instead tried to express the essence of the universe: the truth or the present in all its starkness. But this is not to say that the philosophy of Zen depended on analysis, logic or patterns of thought, for these depend on belief in the individual. In Zen there is no separation between oneself and nature – no supremacy, no fear, just all-encompassing being.

In the Zen tradition, water took on a different form, as did everything. Crystalline and rippled, water was represented by gravel and sand. Surprising as this may seem to western eyes, it is, in fact, quite reasonable. One of the most important characteristics of water is its mobility – a quality of its transience. If one could somehow trap water, so that it remained the same for ever, like concrete unable to change its structure or evaporate, it would lose its magic and become mute, bland and meaningless. Any representation of water is incapable of conveying this quality without cheating. But the Zen Buddhists understood the beauty of the ephemeral and expressed it in their treatment of gravel. Each day the wind and the rain wipe out the delicate traces of sand and gravel, and each day, as part of a Zen exercise, it must be raked and rearranged. The sand and gravel

A graphic design in landscape, the stark formality
of the materials used to contain the stream
creates a jagged cut through a canvas of green.

therefore have something of the transient qualities of water.

Zen gardens show these principles put into practice. One — Daisen-in, in Tokyo — is only 130 yards (119m) square, yet is made up of around 100 stones, representing islands and mountains. Between these, a river of gravel snakes its descent. This is a good example of what the Zen priest Tesen Soki, in his book *Ka Senzui No Fu,* called "reducing 30,000 miles to the distance of a single foot". This symbolism is carried right through the garden: two large upright stones, framed by a soft, leafy halo, represent mountain tops above the clouds; sinuous and determined, the water/gravel crashes against their base before flowing beneath a slab of stone and diffusing into a large expanse of water/gravel dotted with islands/stones. Though treated like a three-dimensional canvas, this masterly work is only about 5.5 yards (5m) wide and 11 yards (10m) long.

Another superb Zen garden can be seen at Ryoanji — though perhaps "garden" is not the correct word, since it contains no plants. It is a rectangle, framed by a rustic wall, that contains 15 stones (considered the ideal number) arranged into five symbolic islands. Green moss covers the islands' slopes, contrasting with the texture and colour of the rippled gravel that carpets the enclosure.

One uses words such as "garden", "wall", "island" and "slope", but this imposes meaning on what is, in fact, a space and no more than a space; Isamu Noguchi, who developed his skills as a sculptor by studying Zen gardens, says "I think of a garden as sculpturing of space". We have given only one interpretation of this space, and there are many others. One is intended to sit on the viewing platform and immerse oneself in the abstraction of the garden, balancing its masses and its relationship with oneself.

The stream of water seems to pierce the glass-like
surface of this charming Koi (carp) pool.

THE MODERN

FROM ARTS AND CRAFTS TO CONSTRUCTIVISM

Approaches to the design of water gardens have varied enormously during the 20th century and have rarely conformed to any universal rules. This seems strange when one considers the artistic unity and resolve of 18th-century landscape designers, and the confidence from which it resulted. But perhaps the greatest influence on modern-day garden design has been the Modern Movement, with its branches, such as Constructivism and Cubism, which has revolutionized all aspects of art and design.

For a time, though, the Arts and Crafts Movement deflected the full force of Modernism. In many ways it was a regression: where the garden had just begun to be treated separately from the house in the 18th century – and even before that at the Villa Lante – the Arts and Crafts Movement made it once more a subsidiary embellishment of architecture, in the same way as furniture is subsidiary to a room.

Gertrude Jekyll and the architect Sir Edwin Lutyens were the main figures in the Movement, together designing more than 100 houses and gardens during the late 19th century and first part of the 20th. Jekyll was highly influenced by Impressionist painters, such as Monet, and reflects this in her sensitive co-ordination of colours and her treatment of plants as living materials for her canvas. Through her, herbaceous borders of large, informally arranged splashes of colour came to replace tidy beds of annuals and roses. It was a return to the rural tradition of intimacy, after the exotic fantasies of Victorian gardeners who filled greenhouses with extraordinary tropical plants and trimmed hedges into extraordinary shapes. And it was also a clear rejection of formal classical architecture and of Capability Brown's landscapes.

Through experimenting in her own garden at Munstead Wood, near Godalming, Jekyll discovered the unique character and artistic potential of different plants during summer and winter. The resulting garden was heralded as an escape from the regimentation and "pastry-work gardening"

The balanced planting and cheeful order of
Abbotswood, designed by Sir Edwin Lutyens and
Gertrude Jekyll.

of the Victorians: in Jekyll's garden one was constantly taken by surprise by what she called "flowery incidents".

Her treatment of water features, however, like that of Lutyens, is simple and reserved, both in terms of their architecture and their functional relationship to plants. She did not favour contrasting the shapes of pools, and so all her designs are rectangular, oval or round. Often the water is raised to the brim of a pool, though, providing a reflection of the house, while an economical placing of aquatic plants — always lilies, in the case of formal pools — softens the edges, provides textural contrast and lends an elegance and tranquillity to the scene. As she says, lilies "would exactly accord with masonry of the highest refinement and with the feeling of repose that is suggested by a surface of still water."

One of Jekyll's most interesting ideas for water design is the use of steps leading into the water. The idea is certainly a good safeguard should children fall into a pool, and the different levels provided by the steps form an ideal base for tiers of lily baskets.

The use of moving water, like that of still water, was also restrained. In fact, on a visit to the Villa d'Este, Lutyens was shocked by the "vulgarity" of its water displays: fountains had no place in Arts and Crafts gardens. Interestingly, though, Lutyens design at Tyringham Park, in Buckinghamshire, was clearly inspired by the elegant Canopus of Hadrian's Villa.

CONSTRUCTIVISM AND THE REJECTION OF ROMANTICISM
After the First World War, the Purist Constructivist movement emerged — even though it was opposed by many. This movement re-defined art and provided a practicable ideology for daily life. Its philosophy was governed by the perception of one reality, existence itself, without distinguishing between the conscious and the unconscious.

In architecture, Constructivism was championed by Le Corbusier and the Bauhaus school, founded by Walter Gropius in Germany in 1919. In sculpture, the leading figures were Ben Nicholson, Naum Gabo, Henry Moore and Barbara Hepworth; in painting, Wassily Kandinsky, Paul Klee, Kasimir Malevich and Diet Mondrian. In landscape design, the leading exponent was Christopher Tunnard (1910 – 1979).

Tunnard's work was fiercely opposed by the Ecologists, who felt that his creations lacked familiarity and intimacy. One of the best examples of it is at Bentley Wood, near Halland in Sussex. The house — built by Serge Chermayeff — and Tunnard's garden effectively define Constructivism.

According to Gertrude Jekyll, lilies "accord with masonry of the highest refinement and with the feeling of repose that is suggested by a surface of still water", as here at Hestercombe.

Tunnard was looking for a substitute for "style and fashion", which the Constructivists felt could never aspire to real art. He dismissed the "pompous anachronism" of the Italian axial vista and the "romantic gesture to the past embodied in the Italianate figure on its pedestal." He wanted to free garden art from tangible connotations and to create a form relevant to a new age with new emphasis on the possibilities of space — no longer to be confined by walls and hedges.

In his book, *Gardens in the Modern Landscape*, Tunnard summarizes his main concern — the function of the garden — with clear references to 18th-century styles and the Arts and Crafts Movement:

"The functional garden avoids the extremes both of the sentimental expressionism of the wild garden and the intellectual classicism of the "formal" garden; it embodies rather a spirit of rationalism and through an aesthetic and practical ordering of its units, provides a friendly and hospitable milieu for rest and recreation. It is, in effect, the social conception of the garden."

Tunnard's second main concern was with Oriental influences. Although his gardens in no way resemble the confined enclosures of Japan, his concept of the garden is similar: the emphasis is on an economy of design components and form. He writes: "we might be content with far less than we ask in garden decoration were we but able to cultivate an empathetic attitude to our material." At Bentley Wood, demonstrating this, the selection of planting materials is limited, but entirely appropriate, and the effect of this economy is to bring out a sculptural quality in the plants.

Others, of course, had relied on sculptural quality, but the main difference between Tunnard and those of his predecessors who did this is his rejection of romantic "nature worship". Whereas his predecessors believed that wild and beautiful countryside inspired man's progress and was therefore in some way superior, Tunnard believed that nature and man should enjoy equal status. So he substituted an intellectual and functional interpretation of nature for a romantic idealization — and it was this that made him so unpopular with the Ecologists.

Tunnard's final concern was with modern art. He had a great dislike for valueless ornament, and strongly emphasized the difference between art and ornament: "The profitless search for decorative beauty, a purely relative quality is abandoned in the creation of the work of art." He stressed the idea that a work of art has importance if it inspires curiosity or thought

Tunnard emphasized the economy of design
elements and form that is a feature of Japanese
gardens, such as this classic example.

in the same way as a symbol. Whether it does this depends, so Tunnard believed, on its purity and the sensitivity with which it is incorporated into surroundings.

But Tunnard's three concepts did not just provide the framework for Constructivist garden design. Their importance also lies in their introduction of the idea that modern art can be transmuted into landscape design.

FRANK LLOYD WRIGHT

The American architect Frank Lloyd Wright was claimed by many as the champion of the Ecological Movement. In 1937, he created *Falling Water*, his most significant work and one that rescued him from what has been described as the nadir of his professional career. But though, as contemporary ecologists claim, it is more sensitive to the environment than Constructivist architecture, it is in fact a powerful response to Le Corbusier's Villa Savoie and shares similar design principles — one Constructivist in essence.

This can be demonstrated by a look at two particular facets of the design: first, the floating terraces supported by a system of cantilevering have a character and form that is the rational result of their desired function and purpose. They therefore avoid conforming to any specific style. Second, the structure spreads out both vertically and horizontally, expressing a relationship with space rather than mass and volume. Both these qualities are typical of Constructivism.

Having said that, *Falling Water* shows an enormous sensitivity in its use of organic material, and offers an intense experience of nature. This experience differs from that offered by the Villa Savoie, in which the experience is primarily one of sky and sun. In *Falling Water* the use of locally quarried stone represents the earth and its growth upwards and outwards to light. At the same time, the ingenious placing of the balconies echoes the waterfalls. The structure is a magical fusion of rock, light and water and transcends what Ecologists think off as the inertia of typical Constructivist building material. It can best be described as Constructivism under the cloak of Romanticism.

LUIS BARRAGAN

One of the most interesting designers of the 20th century, Luis Barragan was born in Mexico in 1902. In the early 1930s he attended Le Corbusier's lectures in Paris, then returned to Mexico, where he designed a number of magnificent buildings and gardens. Though he is better known for his

Frank Lloyd Wright's cantilevered building at
Falling Water blends perfectly with a natural
waterfall.

buildings, Barragan in fact refers to himself as a "landscape architect".

Barragan's work is characterized by a brilliant interplay of planes, colours and shadows, inspired by the red earth, horse troughs and provincial life of his native village. As a result, his designs make use of water in a manner that much of Constructivist architecture lacks.

One of his most interesting works is the *Plaza del Bebedoro de los Caballos*, in Las Arboledas, built between 1958 and 1962. It is nothing more than a long horse trough flanked and shadowed by a row of immense eucalyptus trees. A shadow of one eucalyptus tree is projected onto an enormous, pastel-coloured, free-standing wall to the same scale as the trees. Beyond this, there is a slender blue wall, echoing the colour of the water and creating both a sense of cool and depth. The trough itself is brimming with water and its long flat expanse takes on an abstract quality within the context of these textures.

THOMAS CHURCH AND SIR GEOFFREY JELLICOE

In America, Thomas Church has been a prime source of inspiration for landscape designers. His gardens mark a return to the sensuality of organic curves, in contrast to the rectilinear designs of Constructivism. His famous swimming pool at Sonoma, California, is famous for its perfect, fluid contours and its sensation of embryonic softness. The water is no longer architectural or solid in feeling, but wonderfully tactile.

A similar organic sensation is apparent in the work of the Englishman Sir Geoffrey Jellicoe, who was born in 1900. Jellicoe was strongly influenced by the artists of the Modernist Movement, and tried too achieve a universal harmony in spatial relationships by manipulating shape, symbol and allegory rather than tangible qualities, such as physical mass and volume. In his book, *Studies in Landscape Design*, he quotes the painter Kasimir Malevich as "desperately trying to free art of the useless weight of the object."

So taking account of these Constructivist precepts, Jellicoe began to explore the possibilities of spatial relationships and to work on man's curious appreciation of curvilinear and rectilinear shapes, such as circles, squares or abstractions. In doing so, he evolved a symbolic architectural language with which he attempted to translate these precepts into landscape. At Sutton Place – possibly Jellicoe's most important work – for example, he tried to explore the abstraction of man's deep and enigmatic relationship with landscape without, as he says, "losing touch with the material world", a far cry from Tunnard's "spirit of rationalism".

The Islamic Fountain in the Paradise Garden at
Sutton Place plays an important part in Sir
Geoffrey Jellicoe's life allegory, which runs
through his whole design.

SUTTON PLACE

After the death of Paul Getty, the oil millionaire, Sutton Place, near Guildford, Surrey, was bought by Stanley Seeger, another American. It was under his auspices that Sutton Place truly blossomed, with the culmination of Jellicoe's life's work. Today, Sutton Place is a unique site, and one that has tremendous importance to the modern movement in landscape art. There are several reasons for this: first, the sheer scale of the project; second, the way in which a beautifully preserved 16th-century manor house combines with some of the greatest examples of 20th-century sculpture.

Jellicoe was, perhaps, fortunate, not only in that his materials were of the best, but also that he had the freedom to juxtapose them in such a way as to express one of his fundamental beliefs, as expressed in the *Guelph Lectures on Landscape Design:* "that history is a continuum of the past, present and future, and that an objective in landscape design is not to smother history, but to build on it".

The importance of this concept becomes clear when one looks at Sutton Place. The house itself has hardly been changed since it was built in 1552; The landscape, however, has evolved, mirroring the parallel unfolding of history and evolution of culture. Ironically, though, the English landscape school is not represented at Sutton Place, whose garden has always had a classical feel to it.

According to Jellicoe, the practice of landscape design has been governed throughout history by the opposing poles of classicism and romanticism, or — as some have it — rationality and irrationality, or the eye and the mind. But perhaps those facets of the human mind that might appear to be fundamentally opposed to each other have, from time to time, really been closer than has appeared. The mood of the Renaissance, for example, was to try to sweep away superstition and shadowy fears: what the archaeologist Jacquetta Hawkes described as "the strange, ancient furniture of the unconscious mind". For a time, the furniture was swept away, only to be brought back in even more potent form by the Mannerist Movement. Throughout history, in fact, humans have never quite been able to convince themselves that life and nature can be categorized, let alone understood. Powerful, primeval forces — or, as Coleridge has it, in *Kubla Khan,* "the ancient voices prophesying war" — always seem to be lying in wait, ready to ravage our superficially ordered world.

At Sutton Place, Jellicoe's aim was to release "the un-reasoned fantasies of the sub-conscious" into the ordered classical layout. As he continues in the *Guelph Lectures,* "It would seem that to project into the environment

Inspired by Joan Miro, the abstract sun-raft and
stepping stones give form to the Miro Mirror,
Jellicoe's swimming pool at Sutton Place.

the whole and not merely part of the mind of man, individual or collective, is the highest objective in the creation of landscape as an art."

The final effect is one of complete balance. Neither classicism nor romanticism lends a bias to the essential humanity of Sutton Place. The classical plan, similar to that of an Italian Renaissance garden is interwoven with "irrational incidents". In the same way as at Stourhead, these can be though of as adding up to a grand allegory: at Sutton Place, the allegory is of creation, life and aspirations.

As part of this allegory, Jellicoe used the earth dug during the creation of his lake to form two hills: one represents a father; the other a mother. Between them, a small promontory juts out, breaking the flowing contours of the lake. In the original design, a Henry Moore sculpture was intended to be placed on the promontory, to represent the beginnings of life and civilization: in fact, creation – the first part of the allegory. Another part of the allegory is contained in the Paradise Garden, separated from the east facade of the house by a moat crossed by means of stepping stones. The four arbours and Islamic fountain within the Paradise Garden can thus only be reached after a difficult crossing, which demands resolution and a spirit of enterprise.

The theme of an allegory for life is continued in the Swimming Pool Garden, west of the house. Although most pools are lined with a clinical, white-coloured material, Jellicoe uses a dark shade. This makes the sun-raft and stepping stones stand out in exaggerated relief, their shape and positioning making an emphatic statement on the glassy surface of the water. Called the Miró Mirror, the pool was inspired by the work of the Spanish painter Joán Miró.

But perhaps the final, and most magnificent expression of the life allegory is *White Relief*, and enormous sculpture by the English artist Ben Nicholson. Jellicoe said about it: "I think Ben has brought to earth something of the infinity of the world that lies around us all. This is done in a matter of just a few lines carved out of Carrera marble. No compromise, putting the truth; in fact, let us say you have arrived at the truth".

The marble wall, presumably chosen by the artist, stands round a formal pool specifically designed to catch its full reflection. Its simplicity, and delicacy is ingeniously enhanced by a scattering of lilies.

Unfortunately, Sutton Place is has now closed its doors to the public. Its allegories of life and truth are hidden – but, I hope, will not be hidden indefinitely, for it is always sad to when a work of art cannot be generally enjoyed, and especially so when it is not only the culmination of an artist's

White Relief, Ben Nicholson's awe-inspiring
sculpture in Carrera Marble, poised above its
purpose built pool at Sutton Place.

life's work, but one that combines so many arts to link humanity to time and space in such a unique way.

THE FUTURE

It is difficult to know in what direction landscape art and water gardening will move after Sutton Place. Projects on such a scale require considerable financial resources, and so the direction they take tends to reflect the aspirations and ideas of the person who provides those resources. If, as Jellicoe believes, we have reached a new stage in the union between natural form and art, then even a typical domestic garden could be made into a medium for the highest forms of expression: statement of the abstract language of design, using the ancient form of the water garden.

Vivid laces of water arch over the black monoliths
of this minimalist Japanese garden, giving it an
almost futuristic quality.

WATER GARDEN TECHNIQUES

Formal or informal; Planting and Protection;
What kind of pool?; Shape; Depth; Pool Liners and
Pre-formed Pools; Installation; Edging and Paving;
Building a Bog Garden; Fountains; Waterfalls;
Tsukubai; What Type of Water Feature?; Lighting;
Fish; Planting and Maintenance; Plant Listings.

INDEX and ACKNOWLEDGEMENTS

A simple, Japanese-style bridge can add elegance
and sophistication to any water garden.

FORMAL OR INFORMAL

Introducing a water feature into a garden will breathe new life into it, giving its components, its trees and open spaces, or in a smaller garden, its boundaries and borders, a new visual appeal. In a sense, it dramatizes physical relationships. For this reason it should be handled with confidence and purpose.

The design of a pool is the first and most important step in its creation. Like all design, this includes style, function and desired effect. There are, of course many different styles of pool, but, basically they fall into two broad categories. These are the formal and the informal. Although it is possible to combine the two styles, an informal pool within a formal context or a formal pool within an informal context — this runs the risk of creating a basic

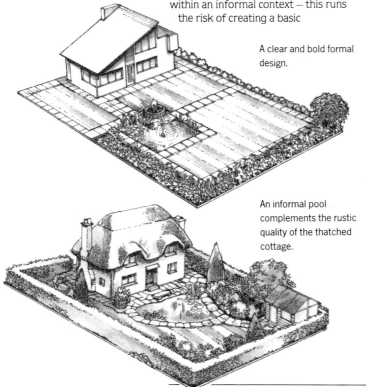

A clear and bold formal design.

An informal pool complements the rustic quality of the thatched cottage.

incompatibility. Therefore when making choices about design, bear in mind the type of home you live in, whether it is a thatched cottage in the country or a modern town house. This consideration will also affect the decision you will have to make as to where you site the pool.

If the pool is to be located near the house, it ought to enhance and dramatize its architectural style. It is possible to juxtapose the energy and severe lines of much modern architecture with the smooth contours of an informal pool. But this would be difficult to achieve with a small pool in a small garden, where it might look diminutive and out of place. It is quite simply a question of scale. In most cases, where the size of the house is relatively much larger than the area taken up by the pool, a geometric house with sharp, crisp lines should be complemented by a formal pool.

If on the other hand you wish to site the pool at some distance from the house, an informal pool might be more suitable. A pool placed at the end of the garden, not visible from the house, will be an interesting discovery on a walk through the garden. Generally, though, the aesthetic and horticultural potential of a garden can be best exploited if the pool is a focal point in the garden.

Unlike the formal pool, the informal pool should not echo modern architectural style. Instead it should suggest a feeling of permanence, of having been formed before the house was built, and in this way it signifies a satisfying link with nature.

PLANTING AND PROTECTION

Having decided on the shape, size and site of the pool, the next question to consider is that of planting. Firstly, should the pool contain planting or not? Beautiful pools exist both with and without plants. There are a few fundamental points to bear in mind. Most aquatic plants will not thrive in the vicinity of fountains or waterfalls, as they dislike turbulence. So if the pond is small, it might not be wise to incorporate a waterfall, or fountain, as well as plants.

Ideally, in order to cultivate healthy aquatics, your pool should fulfill two conditions. It must receive the maximum amount of sun, so ensuring robust growth of plants and optimum flowering and secondly, it should be protected from the wind, which otherwise will snap the tall stems of marginal plants. Preferably the location should be south-facing, with protection from the northerly wind. This protection can be provided by the house or trees. It is important, however, not to site the pool too close to deciduous trees, unless the leaves can be raked out or prevented from falling into the water. Debris from fallen leaves, seeds and twigs will decay and cause pollution. Leaves from holly, laurel and horse chestnut are poisonous and the laburnum highly so. You should also be wary of poplars and willows, however attractive they may appear, as they contain aspirin.

Although the garden designer often hesitates at first about siting a pool in the proximty of the house, this is often the best position. Not only will the house protect the pool from the wind, but you will be able to enjoy the special beauties of the pool from inside your home: the view of slowly unfolding leaves and buds, the shooting flames of fish and dragonflies and the reflections of the changing skies are an unending source of delight.

In the winter, the surface is transformed by the low winter light and sometimes it will freeze over. These variations in the appearance of the water are infinitely compelling. Remember also that in the summer or winter, the steely glint and glass-like texture of the water will emphasize textures and colours in the garden proper. For this reason alone, it is a good idea to place the pool in the line of view from a window.

The ideal site for a pool is a sunny location, sheltered either by the house or by strategically-placed planting. Aquatic plants will achieve optimum performance if the pool is located in a sunny spot with protection from the wind.

WHAT KIND OF POOL?

Raised pools have certain advantages over sunken ones. Although the former can never look totally natural, they can add a distinct touch of style to your garden. In a wet climate, the continual replenishment of a raised pool by rainfall creates an irregular silver patina of raindrops on the water surface, while clouds cause ever-changing reflections. These transformations give the raised pool enormous aesthetic potential. Also, by its very nature, the raised pool gives a greater impression of the physical mass and quantity of water; its containment becomes more significant.

The disadvantage of raised pools is their susceptibility to temperature changes. Artificial insulation certainly helps, but it never matches the stability of earth temperature. The raised pool is perhaps more difficult and expensive to construct, requiring some knowledge of both concrete- and brick-laying, but nothing that could not be mastered by the enthusiastic amateur.

The sunken pool provides ideal conditions for all kinds of vegetation, including a bog garden. The earth that has been dug up can be used to create a mound on which you can build a waterfall and introduce further planting.

The art of creating sunken pools was perfected by the Japanese, who included bridges and islands to reproduce an exquisite minature of the natural landscape. Glimmering lanterns in these quiet gardens give anyone who enters them a feeling that he or she is entering a fantasy world.

The emphasis in the English water garden is different. Its beauty lies in the luxuriant and colourful growth of a rich variety of aquatic plants. To create this sort of garden you will need to acquire a knowledge of different types of plants and their individual needs.

A more formal water garden can offer a surprising range of possible designs. The severity of geometrical lines might appear stark and unnatural to some, but this can be offset by intelligent planting. The handsome leaves of some aquatic plants make an inviting contrast to the precise lines of the pool.

A raised pool can provide a pleasant seating area in the garden.
One advantage of a sunken pool is that it is less susceptible to fluctuations in temperature and guarantees better plant-performance.

SHAPE

A common mistake when designing a pool is to make the shape too complicated. The most obvious disadvantage is that it is harder to build a pool with a complicated shape than it is to build one with a simple shape. There are, however, other problems. Remember, you will never appreciate the view of the garden from an aerial perspective. Therefore the elaborate design on paper will be distorted when looked at straight on. A convoluted design will make the garden appear cluttered. As the plants mature, a "tight" construction may be choked up, losing the comforting glint of water and the shape of the contours. The best policy is to stick to a simple shape.

One of the most efficient ways of deciding on a particular shape is to use a length of rope or hosepipe as an outline for the pool. Take into account the areas which will be in the shade and those in sunlight. Bear in mind that hardy water-lilies will require at least four hours of direct sunlight a day and tropical water-lilies at least five or six. The size should be proportional to the size of the house, garden and other garden features. Even at this early stage, it is important to consider which properties of water you wish to exploit. Every garden has some inherent potential, which a water feature can highlight. A sensitivity to natural form and the different aspects of the garden go a long way towards creating a successful water feature.

By experimenting with the rope or hosepipe, you can get a fair idea of the size of the pool. It is best to make this as large as possible, given the amount of space available overall. The bigger the pool, the more chance it has of achieving a self-sustained ecological balance. This requires a certain stability in temperature, which will be forfeited if the pool is small.

When planning a pool, bear in mind that it will look different when looked at straight on than when seen from above.

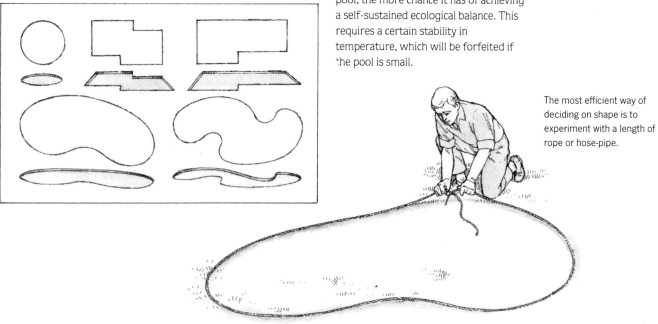

The most efficient way of deciding on shape is to experiment with a length of rope or hose-pipe.

DEPTH

Having decided on the location and general shape of the pool, construction can begin. Here, it is important to understand how depth can affect the health of aquatic plants and fish. Although the pool should be as large as possible – within the limits of your

of 40 foot square should never be less than 15 inches deep. (A pool with a surface area of 4 metres square should never be less than 38 centimetres deep). This means that one square foot will have eight gallons of water beneath it (one square metre should have 380 litres). Anything less than eight gallons per square foot (or 380 litres per square metre) will jeopardise the ecological stability of the pool and discolour the water. If the depth is 24 inches (60 centimetres), every square foot (square metre) of water will constitute 12.5 gallons (600 litres). This would be an excellent depth.

A pool larger than 40 foot square (or four metres square) should be at least 18 inches (45 centimetres) deep and, if over 100 foot square (or 10 metres square), it should be at least 24 inches (60 centimetres) deep. This constitutes 12.5 gallons (600 litres) per square foot which is an ideal volume/surface ratio.

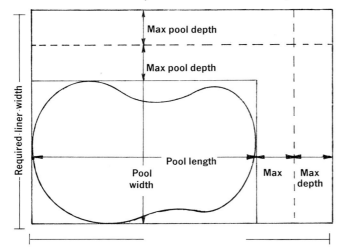

Use this plan to calculate the amount of lining material you will need.

garden – it will rarely be necessary to dig deeper than two feet (60 centimetres).

Depth can be calculated according to the volume of water. If the surface area of the pond is not counterbalanced by adequate depth the pond will overheat. Consequently the water will quickly become a breeding ground for algae, that chokes plants and discolours the water. These problems can be avoided provided the volume of water is adequate. You should aim for at least ten gallons per square foot (490 litres per square metre) – seven (318 litres) at the minimum. A pool with a surface area

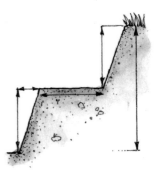

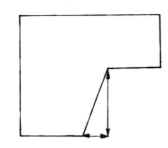

When you have decided the depth of your pool and worked out the angle of slope (*top*), make a template of hardboard or wood to those dimensions (*middle*). Then use this to ensure precise measurments when digging (*bottom*).

POOL LINERS AND PRE-FORMED POOLS

There are a number of different ways of building a pool. Before the advent of concrete and liners, pools were waterproofed with puddled clay, mixed with straw and "puddled" until they became impermeable. With the introduction of concrete, pre-formed pools and liners, waterproofing techniques have become much simpler.

Although it is tempting to have more faith in the strength and durability of concrete than in pre-formed pools and liners, it is possible that stress — the expansion and contraction caused by freezing for example, or by the growth of tree roots — will crack the concrete. The advantages of concrete tend to diminish when compared with a butyl or laminated PVC pool liner, which can be moulded into any shape, is unaffected by temperature fluctuation, ultra-violet rays, oxidising agents and, in the case of butyl, has a life expectancy of up to 100 years. Even if it is punctured it can be repaired.

The best butyl lining is 0.030 inches (0.8 millimetres) thick and comes in black. If the edges are well-made and the lining is not visible, black will bring out the clear reflective properties of a deep pool. If, however, you prefer a shallow effect, butyl is not suitable, so you might consider instead a laminated PVC, which comes in blue.

It is important to know the depth of the pool when calculating the size of the lining. If a pool is 10ft x 10ft x 2ft (3.05m x 3.05m x 0.60m) deep, the lining should measure 14ft x 14ft (4.27m x 4.27m). This is worked out by a simple calculation. Add twice the pond depth, in this case, 2ft x 2ft (0.60m x 0.60m) to both length and width, which makes 14ft (4.27m). If the area is 6ft x 8ft (1.83m x 2.44m) and 18in (46cm) deep, the liner will measure 9ft (2.74m), that is, (6ft + 18in + 18in) (1.83m + 46cm + 46cm) x 11ft (3.35m), that is, (8ft + 18in + 18in) (2.44m + 46cm + 46cm).

The alternative to lining is the pre-formed pool, made from either resin-bonded glass fibre or the less expensive semi-rigid plastic. If the shape, size and depth fit your design requirements, this can be the most convenient way to create a pool. It is a common mistake, however, to choose one for convenience but overlook its limitations.

When visiting a garden centre, it is difficult to envisage exactly how a pre-formed pool will look once it is installed in your garden. Often it will seem bigger seen above ground, than it will when sunk in the pool-site and disguised with plants. Another disadvantage is that you cannot create your own design, and it may be difficult to find one that fits well into the style and shape of your garden.

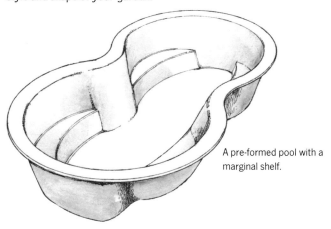

A pre-formed pool with a marginal shelf.

INSTALLATION

Whether you opt for a lining or a pre-formed pool, in both cases you should start the procedure of installing the pool with a template made from wood. This is used to check the level of the marginal shelf and the angle of the pool sides.

The pool sides should not be vertical, since, if they are, they may collapse. The optimum angle is 20 degrees to the vertical or one inch in three. If the soil crumbles easily or if it is sandy, this angle should be increased. The marginal shelf should be about ten inches (25cm) wide and nine inches (23cm) below the edge.

Before you start to dig, it is a good idea to hammer in some pegs to ensure that the sides of the pool will be level. Hammer the pegs down to the level you want the pool sides to be. Using a spirit level and a length of straight wood, make sure all the pegs are exactly the same level. This will prevent one side of the pool from being higher than the other.

Once the desired depth has been reached, any sharp objects on the pool floor should be removed as they might pierce the lining. To safeguard further against this, it is best to put down a ½ inch (12.7mm) layer of sand on the pool floor. The sloping sides can be cushioned with newspaper or roofing felt.

Next the liner can be placed over the hole. Make sure there is an even overlap on all sides, which you then weigh down all around with stones. A constant tension on the liner as it is being filled with water will ensure a minimum of

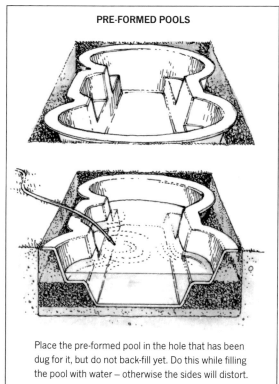

PRE-FORMED POOLS

Place the pre-formed pool in the hole that has been dug for it, but do not back-fill yet. Do this while filling the pool with water – otherwise the sides will distort.

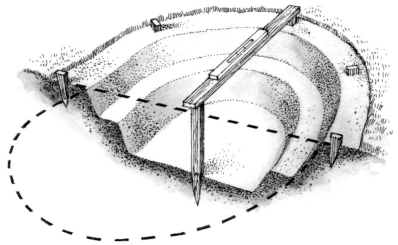

Use a length of straight wood, a spirit level and wooden pegs to ensure the pool is level.

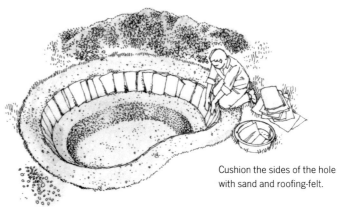

Cushion the sides of the hole with sand and roofing-felt.

creases. At any rate the creases will not be discernible when the plants have matured.

When installing a pre-formed pool, it is important to fill the gap surrounding it with earth, at the same time as you fill the pool with water. Any other method will result in distortion of the pool shape. Choose fine earth rather than coarse, and make sure that it is well pushed in to ensure support for the pool on all sides.

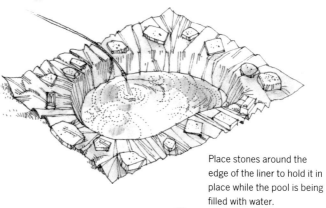

Place stones around the edge of the liner to hold it in place while the pool is being filled with water.

If the pool is raised, the retaining wall must also be lined with butyl.

It looks more attractive if the butyl is run between the two rows of bricks in the wall, but this may make the structure less stable.

A marginal shelf combined with a raised water level gives the pool another dimension.

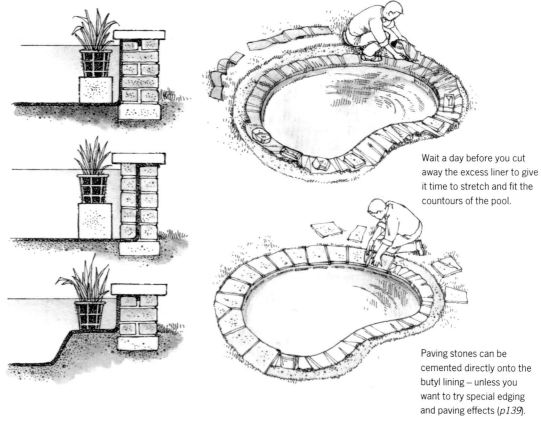

Wait a day before you cut away the excess liner to give it time to stretch and fit the countours of the pool.

Paving stones can be cemented directly onto the butyl lining – unless you want to try special edging and paving effects (p139).

EDGING AND PAVING

A cement foundation for the paving stone increases stability and may be essential in sandy soil. Dig a trench before digging the pool, then: **1** Fix wooden shuttering at a 20 angle. **2** Pour in the cement evenly, making sure it fills all the corners. **3** When the cement is dry, remove shuttering and dig out the pool. **4** When laying the liner, remember to leave a surplus of around 7 inches (18cm).

Building the edging is a very important stage in the construction of the pool as you will have to be aware of both its functional and aesthetic roles. Not only does the edging serve to hide the pool-lining, it also enhances the design. A very simple pool can be made to look something quite special. Edging can also be extended to form an adjacent terrace or, in the case of an informal garden, it can be made to look like a natural slope.

Once the pool is full, the surplus liner should be removed, but remember to leave about 7 inches (18cm) around all the sides. You must be certain that the weight of the water takes up all the

liner, so wait a day or two before cutting it. Once cut, the paving stones can be cemented directly on to the lining. To ensure the paving stones are quite stable, it is best to use large ones, at least 20 inches square (131 centimetres square). Do not forget that you will need a 3-inch (7.6cm) overlap to hide the lining and protect it from the sun. (The overlap also helps to give the pool a look of depth and mystery). The paving should be cemented using a three-part sand to one-part cement mortar. If you want the water to come right up to the paving stones you would do well to mix in an impermeabilising

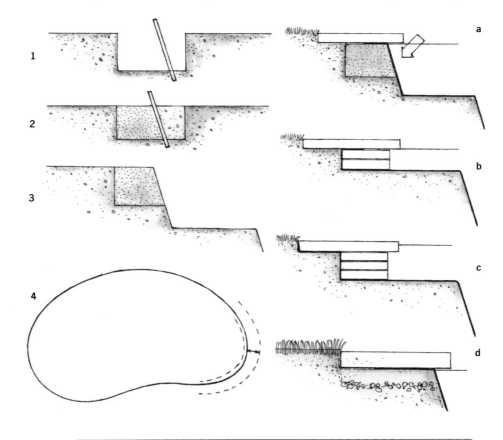

a Position the paving stone so that it just overhangs the water, and protect the cement with the liner.
b For extra protection, wrap the butyl liner round the foundation; if the water level is to be above the foundation, **c**, wrap the underside of the paving stone in liner, too, but if you decide to do this, remember to leave more excess liner before cutting it.
d Planting will help to camouflage the liner when it reaches behind the paving stone.

agent, otherwise the water will leak through the cement. A basic rule to follow is that any cement that will come into contact with water should be treated with either a rubberized paint, or a special chemical, such as *Silglaze*.

If you do not wish to have edging around the pool, you may prefer to build a gentle slope instead. Remember that the angle of the slope will reflect the depth of the pool. A shallow slope suggests a shallow pool and a deeper slope suggests a deeper one. To achieve a perfect balance in which the pool blends in harmoniously with its surroundings you will have to take time to experiment. Remember that planting will make a difference and this should be taken into account when deciding on the angle of the slope.

Interesting paving stones can turn a simple pool into something quite special, as well as hiding ugly linings. Included below are: a variety of brick-patterns, crazy paving, cobble stones and circular slabs nestling in plants.

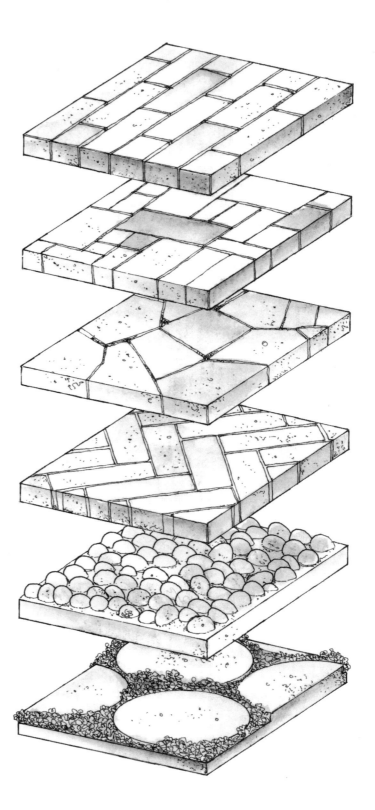

BUILDING A BOG GARDEN

A bog garden is an ideal way of creating a pleasant transition between water and land. As well as providing an interesting visual link in your garden design, it will also give your garden greater horticultural variety. This includes a profusion of weeds. Bog garden plants differ from aquatic plants because their roots need air, so it is one of the great advantages of lining that it makes this possible.

Bog gardens are suitable for both formal and informal pools. A formal pool can be complemented by building a dividing wall at each end creating two narrow beds. A bog garden for an informal pool should bring out the

inherent contours, but this might be difficult after the pool has been made. A bog garden can be built inside or outside the main pool, simultaneously or after its construction, though this has its disadvantages with an informal pool, as stated above. If it is created at the same time, it is a question of sculpting a dividing mound which should then be covered by liner and topped with stone.

If the bog garden is created after the construction of the main pool, a retaining wall must be built, using bricks and mortar, which allows water to permeate through. Since this wall will not have deep, strong foundations, it should have a broad base to prevent it

Formal pool

Bog garden

Informal pool

Bog garden

A bog garden can easily be incorporated into the design of a formal pool by extending the liner and separating main pool from the bog garden by means of a broad-based wall.

With an informal pool, use a dividing wall of large stones.

Perforate the hose pipe supplying the bog garden with regularly spaced holes, to ensure an even supply of water throughout the area.

evaporation that occurs through the bog garden. This means the water level of the main pool will be lowered, so the water will have to be continually replenished. In general, therefore, it is not advisable to build a bog garden in a shallow pool.

A possibly more effective bog garden can be created by digging a completely separate hole, about 18 inches (44cm) deep, next to the main pool. This should be lined with a polythene liner, perforated to prevent saturation and water stagnation, which will sour the earth. Lay 6 inches (15cm) of gravel around a hosepipe perforated with holes 24 inches (60cm) apart. Make sure that the holes are not too big and are regularly sized, as otherwise irrigation will be uneven. The pipe should be sealed at one end with the other end exposed. During summer months it is simple business connecting the hose pipe to a tap and irrigating the bog garden.

A bog garden should have 12 inches (30cm) of soil. If it is to be within the main pool, a bank will have to be built to allow aeration of the roots. The soil mixture should consist of one half loam, or seasoned compost mould, a quarter coarse-grained sand – from two to five millimetres in size to allow permeation – and the rest should be well-rotted cow manure and peat.

collapsing. The wall should be built on a pool liner, which should be protected, using roofing felt or liner. Take care to treat the mortar with *Silglaze* before filling the pool with water as otherwise pollution may result. The bog garden within the main pool is an often criticised technique, because the water of the main pool frequently becomes muddied. Building the wall too high in order to prevent this, is not a solution however, as there will not be enough water to saturate the garden. Another disadvantage is the considerable

FOUNTAINS

Since the earliest gardens, man has sought ways of creating waterfalls and fountains to celebrate the many properties of water. Nowadays, with the help of modern technology, the delight and charm of these special water features are available to everyone with a garden.

In some cases, however, the pool might not be suitable for either waterfall or fountain. Remember that aquatic plants, for example, dislike water currents, and should not be in the proximity of moving water. So, unless the pool is large enough to accommodate both water feature and aquatics, or a separate rim can be installed, a choice has to be made.

You should also consider how the water feature will fit in with the rest of your garden design. The fountain, for example, is an artificial device with a symmetrical spray and it is not always possible to adapt it to informal surroundings. Scale is also an important aspect. A small fountain might be

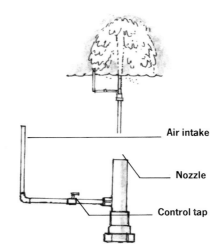

Air intake

Nozzle

Control tap

An aerated jet creates a low mound of foaming water.

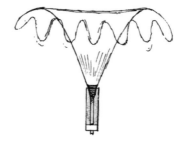

This mushroom jet has a plunger that can be adjusted to vary the height and width of the cascade.

Plunger

With a little skill and imagination, you can bring out the sculptural qualities of a fountain.

depressing in a wet climate, but in a hot climate, the spray is easily evaporated and this causes wastage.

An interesting aspect of the fountain is that it brings out an architectural quality in water. For this reason it often combines well with a hard material like stone.

Modern technology has revolutionized the fountain. Different nozzles can be fitted, that produce a variety of spray patterns. You can buy tinted lenses, which rotate at different speeds, creating kaleidescopic patterns of colour in the water. This technique is particularly effective at night.

Though very spectacular, this kind of fountain will not always fit into the surroundings. It should always be borne in mind that the spirit of water lies in its natural beauty. While special effects, if employed with care and thought, can enhance this beauty, it would be a pity to decorate a water feature like a Christmas tree.

One of the most important practical concerns is the positioning of the fountain. Unless you are careful, wind will blow the spray beyond the perimeter of the pool and create a dangerous, slippery surface on paving, as well as depleting the volume of water in the pool. In order to avoid this, you should ensure that the diameter of the pool is at least twice the height of the jet, and at least four times in windy areas. In the latter case, a straight, columnar jet is never achievable and it would be better to opt for a different form of fountain altogether.

Maintaining a fountain with a small orifice – of the sort that creates a columnar jet – is not always simple, as the smaller the orifice, the more susceptible it is to clogging up. A fountain with a larger aperture produces a lower spray, which falls over a larger area, and is unlikely to become blocked.

Two interesting and unusual designs from Germany show the range of possibilities when building a fountain. One blends traditional and modern (*above*), with water spouting from a pipe into a crude stone basin; the other (*left*) uses high-tech stainless steel discs to obtain its effect.

WATERFALLS

In terms of construction, a waterfall can be divided into a series of descending basins. By planning in this way, each stage of the cascade will provide an individual focus for the eye, while there are other advantages as well. The basins will force the water to pause before each fall, so that the flow leaves the spill edge with constant velocity.

The spill edge is also important visually, as it will shape the form of the falling water. If a jagged surface is used, for example, the sheet will be broken and fragmented. If the surface is fluted, the falling water will be divided into a striated pattern of light and dark.

It is important that the water breaks cleanly with the surface, especially when small quantities of water and slow velocity are involved. Otherwise it will dribble unsatisfactorily and never form a steady sheet. There are two ways of avoiding this. Either the lip can be made of a strip of perspex or metal, which juts out slightly beyond the spill edge, or, the underside of the waterfall can be notched to force a break with the surface tension.

By creating an overhang for each waterfall, you can also amplify the sound of the falling water. The steps of the waterfall should be between 6 and 12in (15 + 30cm) high. If they are any lower neither the sound, nor the vertical movement of the water can be fully appreciated. Experiment with the velocity of the water and plant a rock at the foot of the fall onto which the water can splash. The result will be a pleasant musical sound to back up the waterfall's visual impact and in Japan, indeed, waterfalls are sometimes "tuned" by specialists.

Remember that the higher the source of the waterfall, the stronger the pump required to raise the water. Before deciding on its height it is worth visiting a

The spill edge shapes the flow of water.
A flat edge works better if it has a notch in its under-surface, causing the water to fall freely.
A curling edge creates a sheet flow.

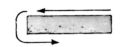

Foliage and roughly-hewn stones make an attractive, natural-looking waterfall.

Remember to line the watercourse with butyl or concrete to prevent leakage.

Careful positioning of stones can turn a simple series of descending basins into an eye-catching waterfall.

pump specialist. The waterfall course should be lined with butyl or concrete, and great care should be taken that it is impermeable. If the liner allows any leakage, the water in the pool that is being recycled will gradually be depleted.

To guarantee efficient waterproofing, it is best to build a reinforced concrete foundation several inches thick, which runs from the source to the pool. Rocks and stones can be added onto this base. As an alternative, butyl can be used, and the stones can be cemented directly onto it. It is also possible to buy moulded glass fibre waterfalls at a water garden centre.

As with a fountain, it is easy to misjudge the correct scale of a waterfall in relation to the garden. To create a sensation of visual depth, place small or angular stones in the background. Like this you can achieve the effect of a fast-flowing mountain stream. Stones in the foreground should be larger and more rounded. You can heighten the visual appeal of a waterfall by conjuring up different moods at different stages.

To create the least possible disturbance to plants the total volume of water per hour should equal the volume of water in the pond. Although twice the volume is acceptable, this will affect the health of the plants. Be careful that the amount of water corresponds to the size of the waterfall. A thin trickle threading its way between large rocks will not be very impressive.

Bearing in mind that the pump will probably not be working all the time, the waterfall should look attractive even when not operative. Perhaps the best way to do this is to create lips for each basin, so ensuring that water remains in them. Liberal sprinklings of gravel will give a textural contrast to the waterfall, even when it is not working. A covering of gravel will also protect the lining from the sun and prolong its life.

Two contrasting styles of waterfall, both quite easy to build. In the traditional style (*left*), undressed stones surround a small, rustic pool, fed by the water from a simple stone channel. A more modern approach (*top*) uses blocks of dressed, metal-strapped stone and metal troughs.

TSUKUBAI

The Japanese *tsukubai* is essentially a stone basin, filled with water and placed beside the path leading to the tea-ceremony house. Washing one's hands in an act of self-purification is one of the integral stages of the ceremony. The idea is similar to the use of holy water in Christian churches.

Nowadays, the tea-ceremony is an exercise in spiritual-training, the purpose of which is to give the participant a heightened perception of beauty. This is achieved through a long and delicate ritual, which is structured around the drinking of a special kind of tea.

Any vessel can be used for the *tsukubai*, though to remain true to the spirit of the ceremony, it should evoke a certain aura of dignity and solemnity. In Japan, such

vessels include foundation- pillars and millstones or hollowed-out rocks. The vessel should be at least 6 inches deep and the water should always be clean.

To appreciate the tea-ceremony fully, it should be approached with an attitude of humility. For this reason, the *tsukubai* is placed low on the ground so that, regardless of social standing, all participants have to stoop down to cleanse themselves. Crouching down on the first stone, which is placed before the vessel, the acolyte reaches out for the bamboo ladle, with which he scoops water and washes each hand in turn before replacing the ladle. To give an air of solidity, it is best if the *tsukubai* looks sunken into the ground.

Between the first stone and the

A *tsukubai* plays an important part in the Japanese tea-ceremony, but can make an attractive feature in any garden. It can be made from a pillar, a millstone or a hollowed-out rock.

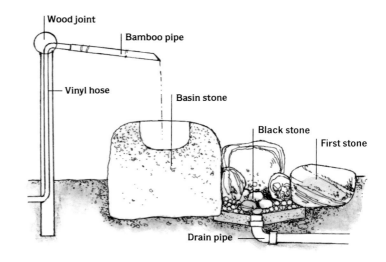

tsukubai is a small rocky hollow, which should be made impermeable and equipped with a drain. The water should never lie still in it and it should be continually cleared of leaves. Both drain and base should be covered with small, round, black stones, which will gleam when splashed with water from the main vessel.

Though there are few examples now, a large urn used to be placed under the drain to catch the water. The sound of a drop splashing on the water within the urn was amplified, so that even though it came from deep below the earth, it sounded uncannily close at hand.

Water is fed into the *tsukubai* through a length of bamboo, which is attached to a garden hose. Make sure the hose is not visible, otherwise the rustic effect will be marred. Alternatively, water can be supplied from the base of the *tsukubai*, creating the effect of a spring. Take care to regulate the flow, so that it does not pour out too forcefully. Often the water is left running so that it looks as if it is emanating from a natural spring. This effect can be enhanced by planting around the bamboo.

The water will flow over the rim of the vessel at one point only, pouring into the rocky hollow at its base. After several years, mosses will begin to grow on the rock, which will add interest to the water feature. Alternatively, you can place the *tsukubai* in the centre of a larger rocky hollow, in which case the water should be made to flow over all sides evenly.

The hollow should be about 6 inches (15cm) deep, and perhaps 16 inches (40cm) in diameter. Using the waterproofing technique discussed above, line the hollow with butyl or cement. Large stones should be placed around the edge and small stones should cover the base. The drain catching the water.

Since the *tsukubai* will probably not be functional outside Japan, elsewhere it must be used in the garden for visual and sound effect. Illumination at night, for example, often works very well.

The *tsukubai* is not difficult to construct, but, as with most water features, a great deal depends on the personal aspirations of the garden designer. Having chosen the vessel, embed it in the earth, so that 8 - 12in (20 - 30cm) remain above ground. Use a spirit level to determine the ideal surface-level of the water, so that it falls down over the chosen side of the vessel. At the same time, you should always try to make the rim appear as level as possible.

The simple outward appearance of a *tsukubai* belies the subtlety and ritual significance of its design.

WHAT TYPE OF WATER FEATURE?

Choose a water feature to reflect the way you feel about your garden. A single-jet fountain, for example, can display a simple elegance that recalls the Islamic tradition of water gardening. A formal pool, on the other hand, can utilize any number of interestiung shapes and patterns; while a Japanese-style garden is easy to create, with the help of some cobble-stones, rocks and a simple bridge.

There is scope for a water feature in almost every type and style of garden, as we have shown in the preceding pages. Assess the particular style of your garden and the space you have available, as well as the feeling you wish to evoke, by referring to them. Then choose whatever type of water feature fits your plan best.

If you choose an Islamic style, for example, remember that it is based on a deep respect for water, and rarely features plants. The shape should be well-defined and formal, and the treatment of water almost abstract. Typically, small Islamic water features include the use of an elegant round basin with a simple fountain, or a millstone on which water forms a thin film. On a larger scale, try creating a pool that resembles the brimming courtyard pool of an Islamic mosque — perhaps softening the design by the restrained use of plants.

A Japanese-style water feature will offer a refined contemplative touch to your garden, and is ideal for a town garden because it can be realized on a small scale. One of the most interesting small features of such gardens is a *tsukubai*, or water basin. As in an Islamic water garden, the structure and beauty of a Japanese garden will depend on inorganic shapes, such as those of rocks.

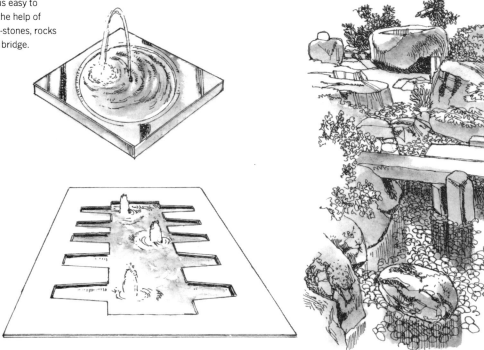

Be sure to introduce a variety of interesting plants into a natural garden.

With surprisingly little water, for example, the effect of a stream can be created by using cobbles for the river bed and rocks to indicate its course. Give the design an idea of movement and space by building a simple stone bridge, and remember to use appropriate accessories: a stone lantern, or perhaps a bamboo fence.

By contrast, an informal water garden can express a love of plants and an intimacy with nature. Informal styles provide great scope for the use of rockeries and waterfalls, but require more space and light than preceding styles. This is because their attraction relies on abstractions, such as the beauty of plants and on the shapes of pools. So consider the surroundings carefully before you decide to build this type of water feature. For example, an informal pool will look strange next to modern architecture unless you make an effort to blend one into the other.

Formal water features can be great fun, because they can incorporate a fountain. There is an enormous choice of designs: large or small, ornamental or plain. So before you start to design a formal water feature, decide whether you want to express dignity and elegance or effervescence and vitality.

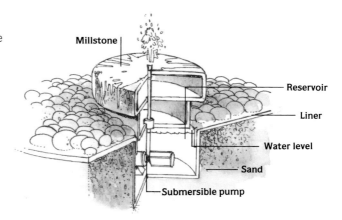

Millstone
Reservoir
Liner
Water level
Sand
Submersible pump

A mill-stone echoes some of the restraint of Islamic garden design when turned into a water feature. Tub gardens are ideal for gardens where space is limited. They are easy to make from barrels or stone basins.

LIGHTING

A light can be an interesting design-feature during the daytime as well as at night.

A sunken light can be made to swivel on an axis.

One mistake, made all too frequently, is to treat lighting as an accessory, when it should be an integral part of any garden design. Think carefully before you position your lights, considering how best you can make the most of your garden's potential during daytime and night-time. However attractive your garden is during the day, effective lighting can help to create a completely different kind of beauty and atmosphere after darkness falls.

Lighting can alter the way a garden is perceived, enhancing already attractive forms and shapes, and disguising less appealing features. In a town garden, for example, you could try to shade out the neighbouring houses. With a little thought, other intrinsic weaknesses in a garden can be turned to advantage in a similar way; with planning, they can even be made to take on a positively romantic allure.

A number of different styles of light are on the market. If you choose carefully, you will find that, far from looking clumsy and out of place during the day, a sequence of lights, thoughtfully placed, makes an interesting design feature and one that contrasts well with the natural environment.

But when a sequence of lights is to be used, try to stick to one common type or shape. This will give the scheme a sense of unity. Be careful, though, that you do not overdo the lighting. Like any component in the garden, lighting should not be used frivolously: each light should either focus on a specific feature or illuminate an obstacle that might otherwise be difficult to negotiate — steps, or a pathway, for example.

Ornamental lighting can be used in a variety of ways. Try directing a light into the trees, to create a wonderful dappled effect; or experiment by covering your lights with perforated shapes.

Make the most of the effect of light on water, by illuminating waterfalls and fountains. If a light is placed so that it shines from below the water surface (take care, because special, heavily insulated fittings are needed for this) it will be captured within the water, forming a dramatic white plume or sheet against a dark background. In still water, this arrangement can be used to make a feature of the submarine world of aquatic plants and fish.

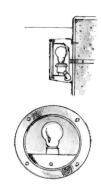

Remember that underwater lights will require special, heavily insulated fittings.

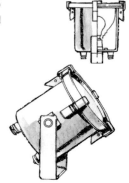

Spotlights can be used to draw attention to the most attractive features in the garden.

An illuminated jet is created by placing the light directly under the fountain.

FISH

The vivid colour and movement of fish add another rich dimension to the pool, embuing its placid surface with life and lending mystery to its hidden depths. One of the results of looking after fish, will be a healthy pool environment. Fish control aquatic insect life, which damages leaves; they also eat the larvae of annoying mosquitoes.

Fish do not, in fact, need much care and attention. Their requirements are sufficient food, plant protection, and well-oxygenated water. Care must be taken that the water is not polluted by dissolved metal ions, which might react if the piping is new, and also that there is no chance of weedkiller poisoning the pool. Cement can also harm fish if it is not treated with *Silglaze*.

It is important not to over-stock the pool, as this will result in a lack of oxygen and also a build-up of poison through waste excretion. For this reason, it is recommended that for every square foot (0.093 metres square) of water, 2 inches (6 centimetres) of fish is acceptable.

It is best to wait a month before stocking the pool to allow the water to establish ecological stability and to give the oxygenating plants a chance to root. (*See Planting and Maintenance*). You should introduce the fish in two stages, to see how they adapt to pool-conditions.

When choosing fish, look out for healthy specimens. Select active fish with erect dorsal fins. Do not choose fish with rotted fins. White spots indicate a fungal disease, which might be a result of damage, and although not contagious, afflicted fish should be avoided.

The most popular varieties of fish include the Goldfish, Shubunkin, Comet and Golden Orfe. Unlike the other three, the Orfe is not a variety of Goldfish. It is an excellent pond-fish, providing lively surface entertainment as well as snapping up insect life.

Fish food comes in either pellets or flakes. Pellets are preferable as they float, attracting the fish up to the surface of the water. If feeding takes place at a regular hour, the fish soon become tame and will gather at the pool-side. The quantity of food depends on the time of year, and it is advisable to consult your supplier. Generally speaking, however, fish will require feeding three times a day during the summer, slightly more frequently during the autumn, and more often again in winter.

Fish will need protection from the sun on hot days, and this can be provided by lilies. Oxygenators are also useful to protect eggs, which can be laid in the foliage. For this reason, you should wait before trimming the plants, until the eggs have hatched.

All sorts of aquatic life add interest to the pool and help maintain a healthy ecological environment.

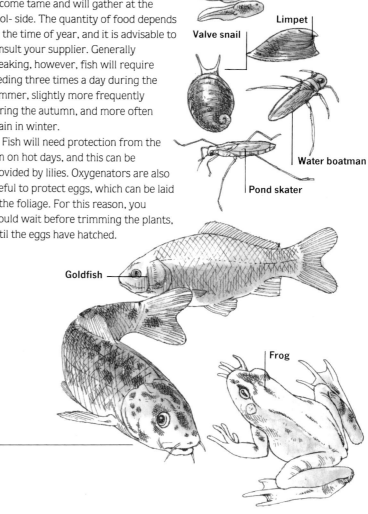

Snail

Tadpole

Valve snail

Limpet

Water boatman

Pond skater

Goldfish

Frog

PLANTING AND MAINTENANCE

Plant water lilies in perforated containers, to ensure maximum health and easy maintenance.

Marginals and oxygenators, too, can be planted in containers, by the water and in it, to give a splash of colour and life to a water feature.

It is more convenient to plant aquatic plants and marginals in containers, than to fill the entire pool with soil, as this causes maintenance problems. The more voracious plants will start taking over the pool and it is an unpleasant job trying to extricate and divide them. Disturbing the pool floor will also sully the water. It is therefore best to plant in movable containers, which are fixed with earth and raised on bricks to the suitable planting depth, (*see plant index*). This method is a much more convenient means of maintainance, since the containers are easily accessible, making plant division and earth changing – which should be carried out every few years – a simple procedure.

The best kind of container is a wide and shallow plastic vessel, perforated to allow movement of water. Cement containers are difficult to move and should not be used unless treated with *Silglaze*. The container should be filled with a loamy soil mixture, as used in the bog garden. You can add a small amount of seasoned fertilizer or bonemeal to this mixture, but take care not to pollute the water with the wrong kind of fertilizer, as this will sour the water and might also affect the food chain.

LILIES

Like all aquatic plants, lilies should be planted when the water has warmed up a bit, so the correct time will vary according to climate. The growing point or "nose" should protrude slightly from the soil, and then the remaining soil surface should be covered with a layer of gravel. This anchors the plants and prevents them from being disturbed by fish. The container should be thoroughly soaked before being sunk into the water to prevent air bubbles from disrupting the soil and muddying the water.

MARGINALS

Marginals can be planted in the same way as lilies. It is a good idea to plant each marginal in a separate container, in order to protect weaker plants from competition from stronger ones.

Iris

Sagittaria

Nymphaea Helvola

Nuphar

Ranunculus

OXYGENATORS

Oxygenators are easy to plant, as their roots do not need to be embedded in the soil. Place them in containers and weigh them down, using a strip of lead or wire so that they do not float about. Be careful not to leave them to long in the sun, out of water, as they will dry up quickly.

MAINTENANCE

A pool is not difficult to maintain, provided an ecological balance is established. This takes about a month. As water in most newly filled pools is alkaline, chemical changes will turn the water cloudy. Then, as algae thrives in alkaline conditions, the water will turn green. As the aquatic plants mature, the water will become acid and the algae coloration will diminish until the water becomes clear.

As mentioned above, it will be necessary to divide the water lilies and thin the oxygenators, in order to prevent them becoming too invasive. The latter may be broken up by hand, but preferably use a pair of scissors. Cut away about a third of the plant, taking care to leave the healthiest looking areas. Water lilies should be divided, every three or four years, when there is too much leaf growth and too few flowers. You should divide the lilies in late spring by slicing through the tuber.

Orontium aquaticum

The divided rootstock, or rhizome, can be replanted, but first the thick and hairless anchor roots can be cut off, as they serve no purpose. Nutrition is absorbed through the slender roots which have small black roothairs.

You should also divide marginal plants. To do this, you simply prise the root apart, using a small handfork.

In autumn, the horticulturalist's water feature will begin to look sad. The leaves and stems will turn brown and sag in the water. The best thing to do is to clear the pond of dead foliage and dredge out the fallen leaves, which will otherwise decompose in the water, releasing noxious gases and causing considerable discomfort to fish.

If there are trees near the pool, it is best to lay some netting over it. This will also discourage predators, such as herons or gulls. The dead leaves and stalks of the marginal plants should be cut back and burnt.

In the winter months, icing over can be a problem. The expansion and contraction of ice will crack cement pools. To prevent this, place a piece of wood or a soft ball on the surface of the water. Fish will also suffer if the surface is completely iced over, and you need to make a hole to allow them to breathe. This is a simple process of pouring boiling water over an area of the ice.

Excessive cold will not harm the plant life, as long as it is covered by at least nine inches (23 cm) of water. Tropical water lilies might need winter protection, in which case they should be lifted, drained and protected with moss, leaves and branches. Other plants, which cannot winter outside, should be lifted and kept in water in a cool place until springtime.

Bulrushes can make a striking feature in a water garden. Sometimes growing higher than a person, they flower in July and August, growing characteristic cylindrical reddish-brown spikelets.

SELECTIVE PLANT LIST

There is an enormous variety of water lilies. When choosing water lilies for your pool, there are a few basic rules to follow. Firstly, much will depend on its size; water lilies with large spreads will choke a small pool. As you should hope to cover between a half and two thirds of the water surface, a 50ft square pool will need about 30ft square of plant cover, (a four metre square pool should have approximately two and a half metres square cover). This area can then be allocated plants from groups A to F, below. The lilies should be chosen for the colour and shape and shape of their leaves as well as their flowers. Remember that sun is a prerequisite for optimum flowering. Hardy water lilies require four hours of direct sunlight a day, while tropical water lilies need five to six.

The following list is categorized according to planting depth and size of spread. Note that the planting depth refers to the distance from the water level to the earth level.

	GROUP NAME	SIZE OF PLANT	DESCRIPTION
	The prefix N refers to the generic name Nymphaea		
A	**N. Pygmaea alba**	3-9 inch depth (approx. 8-23 cm) 1.5 foot spread (approx. 45 cm)	Tiny one-inch white flower. Seed germinates freely.
	N. Pygmaea helvola	3-9 inch depth (approx. 8-23 cm) 1.5 foot spread (approx. 45 cm)	Canary yellow flower with olive green leaves mottled with reddish brown dots.
	N. Pygmaea rubra	3-9 inch depth (approx. 8-23 cm) 1.5 foot spread (approx. 45 cm)	Blood red flower with purplish green foliage larger than either alba or helvola.
	N. Mexicana	3-9 inch depth (approx. 8-23 cm) 1.5 foot spread (approx. 45 cm)	Yellow flower with purple mottled leaves and a reddish underside. It stands several inches above the ground.
B	**Laydkeri lilalea**	5-12 inch depth (approx. 13-30 cm) 2 foot spread (approx. 60 cm)	Pink flower.
	Aurora	5-12 inch depth (approx. 13-30 cm) 2 foot spread (approx. 60 cm)	Yellow flower which matures into orange and finally dark red.

GROUP NAME	SIZE OF PLANT	DESCRIPTION
C **N. Laydekeri fulgens**	7-15 inch depth (approx. 18-38 cm) 3 foot spread (approx. 90 cm)	Crimson flowers with reddish centres.
N. Froebeli	7-15 inch depth (approx. 18-38 cm) 3 foot spread (approx. 90 cm)	Similar to fulgens but flowers have an orange centre.
N. Laydekeri purpurata	7-15 inch depth (approx. 18-38 cm) 3 foot spread (approx. 90 cm)	Deep crimson purple with orange centre and whitish tints on the petals.
N. Graziella	7-15 inch depth (approx. 18-38 cm) 3 foot spread (approx. 90 cm)	Orange blossoms.
N. Hermine	7-15 inch depth (approx. 18-38 cm) 3 foot spread (approx. 90 cm)	Pure white star-shaped flowers with beautiful leaves.
D **N. James brydon**	9-18 inch depth (approx. 23-46 cm) 4 foot spread (approx. 120 cm)	Rose pink flowers with deep orange centres and dark circular leaves. Will tolerate a little shade.
N. Albatross	9-18 inch depth (approx. 23-46 cm) 4 foot spread (approx. 120 cm)	Large white flowers with purple leaves maturing to a bright green.
N. Rose arey	9-18 inch depth (approx. 23-46 cm) 4 foot spread (approx. 120 cm)	Long pointed pink petals.
E **N. William falconer**	9-24 inch depth (approx. 23-60 cm) 5 foot spread (approx. 150 cm)	Crimson red flowers with dark handsome leaves.
N. Gonnêre (also known as snowball)	9-24 inch depth (approx. 23-60 cm) 5 foot spread (approx. 150 cm)	Large pure white 5-6 inch (13-15 cm) dense flowers.
N. Paul hariot	9-24 inch depth (approx. 23-60 cm) 5 foot spread (approx. 150 cm)	Apricot yellow flowers change to orange pink before deepening to red. Maroon mottled foliage.
F **N. Conqueror**	12-30 inch depth (approx. 30-75 cm) 6 foot spread (approx. 180 cm)	Crimson blossoms that flower profusely.
N. Amabilis (also known as pink maruel)	12-30 inch depth (approx. 30-75 cm) 6 foot spread (approx. 180 cm)	Salmon pink flowers mature into a rose pink.
N. Marlialea chromatella	12-30 inch depth (approx. 30-75 cm) 6 foot spread (approx. 180 cm)	6-7 inch (15-18 cm) soft yellow flowers which open later in the day. It will tolerate shade.
N. Escarboucle	9-24 inch depth (approx. 23-60 cm) 5 foot spread (approx. 150 cm)	Large bright crimson blooms, yellow tipped with reddish stamens.
Other surface plants		
Nymphoides peltata		3 inch (7.6 cm) bright green mottled leaves with dainty yellow flowers standing a few inches above water. As it is invasive, it ought to be ruthlessly pruned.

NAME	SIZE OF PLANT	DESCRIPTION
Nuphars		The leaf shape similar to **nymphaea.** Except for **nuphar pumila**, not suitable for pools. Has the advantage of growing in moving water. Inconspicuous yellow flowers from June to August and oval leaves.
Adonegeton distachyus		Water hawthorn, best alternative to water lily tolerating moderate shade. White-lobed flowers with a black stamens have strong vanilla scent and flower even during mild winters. Oblong leaves. Any depth.

OXYGENATING PLANTS

The submerged oxygenating plants are integral to pool life creating clear algae-free water. Without them, microscopic life would soon saturate the pond water turning it green. Oxygenating plants, a more evolved form of life, efficiently extract the mineral salts from the water, depriving algae of nutrients. At the same time they provide necessary shelter, food and oxygen for fish. A pool under 100 ft square will require a bunch for every two foot square. (A pool 10 metres square will need a bunch for every one third of a square metre.) If the pool size is over 100 foot square it will require less. Oxygenators should never exceed one third of the pool's surface area. Though generally forming a carpet, some do have visible flowers. The most popular forms include:

NAME	SIZE OF PLANT	DESCRIPTION
Elodea canadensis (Canadian pondweed)		– a free-floating dark green dense carpet which is easily cropped by hand. It produces tiny flowers from May to October, which according to a South African cookery book, can be used to flavour meat dishes.
Hottonia palustris		– Water violet with 8-16 inch (20-40 cm) spikes of pale mauve flowers from May to August. Light green feathery foliage. It requires partial shade and prefers soft water and acid soil.
Ranunculus aquatilis		– mass of one inch white flowers with gold centres from May to August. Dark green foliage.
Ceratophyllum demersum (hornwort)		Non-rooted dark green feathery foliage on brittle stems which is easily controlled. It requires sun and depth.
Lobelia dortmanna (water Lobelia)		An evergreen, entirely submerged plant with long thin leaves and small light blue flowers.

NAME	SIZE OF PLANT	DESCRIPTION
Calla palustris (bog arum)	Height 6 inches (approx. 15cm) P.D 2-6 inches (approx. 5-15cm)	— Ground-covering spreader with glosy leaves and white sheath-like flowers in May or June. Red berries herald the autumn. Requires a lime-free soil.
Catha palustris (mark marigold)	Height 1-2½ feet (approx. 30-75cm) Shallow water and? mud	— Large golden flowers from March to July with attractive round, veined leaves.
Iris kaemferi (Japanese iris)	Height 36 inches (approx. 90cm)	— Exotic plant with a variety of subtle colours. Prefers water in the growing season but not in winter. Alkaline soil is fatal.
Iris laevigata (water iris)	Height 2 feet (approx. 60cm) P.D 2-5 inches (approx. 20-30cm)	— Lavender blue flowers in early summer. White, pink, yellow cultivars have been produced.
Orontium aquaticum (golden club)	Height 10 inches (approx. 25cm) P.D 6-12 inches (approx. 15-30cm)	— Orchid-like mottled yellow flowers from July onwards.
Pontederia cordata (pickerel)	Height 20 inches (approx. 50cm) P.D 6-12 inches (approx. 15-30cm)	— Blue flower spikes in the late summer and big clumps of spear-shaped waxy green leaves on long stalks.
Sagittaria sagittifolia (common arrowhead	Height 2-3 feet (approx. 60-90cm) P.D 4-6 inches (approx. 10-15cm)	— White flowers with purple centres and distinctive three-pointed leaves — hence "arrowhead". Flowers in July and August.
Scirpus zebrina (zebra rush)	Height 3-4 ft (approx. 90-120cm) P.D 6-12 inches (approx. 15-30cm)	— Distinctive green and white striped leaves. Occasional plain green stems should be cut out.
Typha minima (reed mace)	Height 1½ feet (approx. 46cm) P.D 3-6 inches (approx. 8-15cm)	— Shortest of the typha family. With bluish green spiky leaves and brown pokers.

Waterside plants

Marginal plants will be planted outside the water limit. Common yet striking plants in this category include Astilbes, Hostas, Primulas and Irises.

Astilbe and **Arendsii**	Height 2-3 feet (approx. 60-90cm)	— Refers to a group of cultivars with richly coloured plumes and delicate foliage. Flowers from June into August.
Hosta	Height 20 inches (approx. 50cm)	— Bold luxuriant foliage plants which will not tolerate excesssive sun. flowers in the summer. Their leaves are susceptible to slugs.
Primulas	Varying height	— Drumstick or candelabra species with flowers appearing in tiers. Colours vary greatly. Flower in the summer. These plants prefer acid soil.
Iris sibirica	Height 3 feet (approx. 90cm)	— Many varieties of blue, purple and white flowers forming dense clumps of grassy foliage. Flowers in the summer. Though a waterside plant, it will adapt to drier conditions.

INDEX

ACKNOWLEDGEMENTS

Morgan Samuel Editions would like to thank the following persons and organizations, to whom copyright in the photographs noted belongs:

Cover Cover Tatsui Takenosuke
86 Clive Boursnell; **11** Clive Boursnell; **13** Clive Boursnell; **15** Clive Boursnell; **17** Clive Boursnell; **19** Clive Boursnell; **21** Clive Boursnell; **23** Tatsui Takenosuke; **25** Tatsui Takenosuke; **27** Clive Boursnell; **29** Clive Boursnell; **31** Ken Nakajima; **33** Ken Nakajima; **35** Geoffrey Collens, Derek Lovejoy & Partners; **37** Heather Angel; **39** William Rae-Smith; **40** Clive Boursnell; **43** Spectrum; **45** Robert Harding; **47** Spectrum; **49** Spectrum; **51** Robert Harding; **53** Robert Harding; **55** Ardea; **57** Hutchinson; **59** Impact Photos; **61** Robert Harding; **63** William Rae-Smith; **65** Anne Moorsom, Landscape Institute; **67** Spectrum; **69** Spectrum; **71** Kim Wilkie; **73** Robert Harding; **75** Robert Harding; **77** Hutchinson; **79** Spectrum; **81** Clive Boursnell; **83** Clive Boursnell; **85** Clive Boursnell; **87** Clive Boursnell; **89** Clive Boursnell; **91** Clive Boursnell; **93** Heather Angel; **95** Heather Angel; **97** Heather Angel; **99** Tony Stone; **101** Tatsui Takenosuke; **103** Tatsui Takenosuke; **105** Tatsui Takenosuke; **107** Tatsui Takenosuke; **109** Tatsui Takenosuke; **111** Tatsui Takenosuke; **113** Heather Angel; **115** Garden Picture Library; **117** Tatsui Takenosuke; **119** Robert Harding; **121** Clive Boursnell; **123** Clive Boursnell; **125** Clive Boursnell; **127** Tatsui Takenosuke; **128** Tatsui Takenosuke.

The author wishes to thank Masaru and Naoko Isobe, Tatsui Takenosuke, Ken Nakajima, the Royal Institute of British Architects, the Royal Horticultural Society and Derek Lovejoy & Partners for their invaluable help.